The 9/11 HIJACKERS AND CONSPIRATORS

American Airlines Flight 11—North Tower of the World Trade Center

Mohamed Atta	Hijacker (Pilot)
Abdul Aziz al Omari	Hijacker
Waleed al Shehri	Hijacker
Satam al Suqami	Hijacker
Wail al Shehri	Hijacker

American Airlines Flight 77—Pentagon

Hani Hanjour	Hijacker (Pilot)
Khalid al Mihdhar	Hijacker
Majed Moqed	Hijacker
Nawaf al Hazmi	Hijacker
Salem al Hazmi	Hijacker

United Airlines Flight 93—Pennsylvania

Ziad Samir Jarrah	Hijacker (Pilot)
Saeed al Ghamdi	Hijacker
Ahmed al Nami	Hijacker
Ahmad al Haznawi	Hijacker

United Airlines Flight 175—South Tower of the World Trade Center

Marwan al Shehhi	Hijacker (Pilot)
Mohand al Shehri	Hijacker
Hamza al Ghamdi	Hijacker
Fayez Banihammad	Hijacker
Ahmed al Ghamdi	Hijacker

Other Conspirators Involved with the Visa Process

Khalid Sheikh Mohammed	Mastermind
Tawfiq bin Attash (Khallad)	Potential Pilot
Ramzi Binalshibh	Potential Pilot
Zakariya Essabar	Potential Pilot/Hijacker
Saeed "Jihad" al Ghamdi	Potential Hijacker
Mushabib al Hamlan	Potential Hijacker
Ali Abdul Aziz Ali	Financial Facilitator and Potential Hijacker

Other Conspirator Involved with the Visa and Port of Entry Process

Mohamed al Kahtani	Potential Hijacker

2
The September 11 Travel Operation

The success of the September 11 plot depended on the ability of the hijackers to obtain visas and pass an immigration and customs inspection in order to enter the United States. It also depended on their ability to remain here undetected while they worked out the operational details of the attack. If they had failed on either count   entering and becoming embedded   the plot could not have been executed.

Here we present the facts and circumstances of the hijackers' travel operation, including their 25 contacts with consular officers and their 43 contacts with immigration and customs authorities. We also discuss the 12 contacts with border authorities by other September 11 conspirators who applied for a visa. The narrative is chronological, retracing the hijackers' steps from their initial applications for U.S. visas, through their entry into the United States, to their applications for immigration benefits, and up through their acquisition of state identifications that helped them board the planes. Along the way, we note relevant actions by U.S. government authorities to combat terrorism. There were a few lucky breaks for U.S. border authorities in this story. Mostly, though, it is a story of how 19 hijackers easily penetrated U.S. border security.

Overview of the hijacker's visas

The 9/11 hijackers submitted 23 visa applications during the course of the plot, and 22 of these applications were approved. The hijackers applied for visas at five U.S. consulates or embassies overseas; two of them were interviewed. One consular officer issued visas to 11 of the 19 hijackers. Of the eight other conspirators in the plot who sought visas, three succeeded, but only one of the three later sought to use the visa to enter the United States.

Hijackers Nawaf al Hazmi and Khalid al Mihdhar were the first to submit visa applications because they were originally slated to be pilots. The four hijackers who did become pilots applied for visas in 2000. The remaining "muscle" hijackers applied in the fall of 2000 through the spring and summer of 2001, three applying twice.

Most of the hijackers applied with new passports, possibly to hide travel to Afghanistan recorded in their old ones. It is likely that many of the hijackers' passports contained indicators of extremism or showed ties to al Qaeda. However, this intelligence was not developed prior to 9/11, and thus State Department personnel reviewing visa applications were not trained to spot these indicators of a terrorist connection. Visa decisions for the hijackers and conspirators were consistent with a system that focused on excluding intending immigrants and depended on checking a database of names to search for criminals and terrorists.

Overview of the hijackers' entries

The hijackers successfully entered the United States 33 of 34 times, with the first arriving on January 15, 2000, at Los Angeles International Airport. All others entered through airports on the East Coast, including 11 entries through New York area airports and 12 through Florida airports.

The four pilots passed through immigration and customs inspections a total of 17 times from May 29, 2000, to August 5, 2001. Ziad Jarrah was the most frequent border crosser, entering the United States seven times. Mohamed Atta and Marwan al Shehhi came in three times each, entering for the last time on May 2 and July 19, 2001, respectively. Hani Hanjour was the only hijacker to enter on an academic visa, arriving on December 8, 2000. He had already attended both English and flight training schools in the United States during three stays in the 1990s. Hanjour was also the only pilot who already had a commercial pilot's license prior to entry, having acquired it in 1999 in Arizona.[1]

Though Khalid al Mihdhar and Nawaf al Hazmi came to the United States as early as January 2000, the remaining muscle entered between April 23, 2001, and June 29, 2001. They arrived in six pairs and one trio. Four pairs were processed by the same immigration inspector. Only three of the muscle were referred to a secondary inspection for further scrutiny. Of these, only one, Mohamed al Kahtani, was refused entry to the United States.

Entering the United States as tourists was important to the hijackers, since immigration regulations automatically guaranteed tourists six months of stay. Thus the 14 muscle hijackers who entered the United States in the spring and early summer of 2001 were able to remain in the country legally through September 11. The six-month tourist stays also assured the hijackers of sufficient time to make such preparations for their operation as obtaining the identifications some of them used to board the planes on September 11. Fourteen of 15 operatives and all of the pilots acquired one or multiple forms of U.S. state-issued identification. Only Satam al Suqami did not, possibly because he was the only hijacker who knew he was out of immigration status: his length of stay end date of May 20, 2000, was clearly inserted in his passport.

Note: Per an agreement with the Department of State, we have protected the identities of individual consular officers involved with the adjudication of visas to the hijackers. Throughout the chronology, each is referred to as "he," regardless of the person's actual gender. For similar reasons, we have chosen not to include the names of border inspectors in this report.

The Entry of the Hijackers: Acquiring Visas

November 1998. Upon the indictment of Usama Bin Ladin on November 4, a threat advisory was immediately sent by the headquarters of the Immigration and Naturalization Service (INS) to all immigration inspectors at ports of entry. Warning of possible infiltration into the United States by radical Islamic fundamentalists sympathetic to UBL, the advisory called for "hard" inspections of certain visitors from Middle Eastern countries, but only if they were referred to a secondary immigration inspection. This instruction applied to the countries of origin of all of the hijackers.[2]

April 1999

 On April 3, Nawaf al Hazmi applied for a B-1/B-2 (tourist/business) visa in Jeddah, Saudi Arabia, submitting a written visa application, his passport, and a photograph. Hazmi was a Saudi citizen born August 9, 1976.[3] Hazmi's passport was new--issued on March 21, 1999, and it contained an indicator of extremism that has been associated with al Qaeda.[4]

Also on **April 3**, 1999, the same day that Nawaf al Hazmi was applying for his visa in Jeddah, another of the 9/11 conspirators, **Khallad,** attempted to get a visa in Sanaa, Yemen, using the alias Salah Saeed Mohammed Bin Yousaf. He submitted a written application, a photograph, and a Yemeni passport, issued March 18, 1999, shortly before he applied for this visa. On his application, he listed his date of birth as January 1, 1974, and his nationality as "Yemeni."[5]

Khallad listed his address in the United States as "Bothell W.A.," and gave "Medical Treatment" as the purpose of his visit. Injured while fighting in Afghanistan, he had an artificial right leg. He indicated that he intended to arrive in the United States in April 1999 and stay for a period of "aprox two months."[6]

Khallad was interviewed, apparently by a consular officer, who took notes of their conversation on the visa application. As best as we can tell from the copy we have obtained, the officer wrote "Family in Shobanah and Br (unintelligible)   1 kid   has shops w/family   artificial leg   needs all med info." He denied the application under Immigration and Nationality Act (INA) section 221(g), the provision used to cover denials for incomplete applications or other unspecified reasons, seemingly out of concern that Khallad needed to present more information about his medical condition before he could secure a visa. In general, Yemenis had greater difficulty than wealthier Saudis convincing consular officers they were not intending immigrants.[7]

This is the only visa application we have located for Khallad, though he claims to have applied for one previously.[8]

April 7. Khalid al Mihdhar applied for a B-1/B-2 (tourist/business) visa in Jeddah, Saudi Arabia, submitting a written application, his new passport, and a photograph. Mihdhar was a Saudi citizen born May 16, 1975.[9] Mihdhar's passport was issued on April 6, 1999.[10] Mihdhar's passport contained the same indicator of extremism as Nawaf al Hazmi's. But because this indicator of extremism was unknown at the time to U.S. intelligence officials, the consular officer adjudicating their visas had not been warned to watch for it.

Both Hazmi and Mihdhar's visa applications were destroyed before September 11, according to routine State Department document destruction practices in place in Jeddah, so we could not review them. The electronic records of their applications, their photographs, and information about the visas issued to them still exist, however, and are maintained in the State Department's Consular Consolidated Database (CCD), and we have reviewed this material.

It is not possible to state with certainty whether either Hazmi or Mihdhar were interviewed by a consular officer in connection with their visa applications.[11] The consular officer who approved Hazmi's visa stated, "I do not remember these specific applications."[12] State Department computer records did not provide any help in this regard, because they do not indicate whether the applicant has been interviewed.[13]

If either of these two were interviewed, they must have convinced the officer they had good reasons to be going to the United States: both were issued visas after CLASS record checks showed no derogatory information about them. Hazmi's visa was issued on April 3, 1999. Mihdhar's visa was issued on April 7, 1999. Both were one-year, multiple-entry visas.

January 2000

January 15. **Nawaf al Hazmi** and **Khalid al Mihdhar** arrived together at Los Angeles International Airport from Bangkok, Thailand. The two Saudis were admitted as tourists for six-month stays by the same primary immigration inspector, who was unaware of the indicators of extremism likely present in their passports.[14]

Neither Hazmi nor Mihdhar was on the watchlists available to border inspectors. However, Mihdhar was a known al Qaeda operative at the time, and a copy of his passport was available to the intelligence community.[15]

January 18. **Marwan al Shehhi**, an Emirati, was issued a ten-year B-1/B-2 (tourist/business) visa in Dubai, United Arab Emirates.[16] Shehhi submitted a new passport with his visa application. Although his application was destroyed prior to September 11, 2001, pursuant to routine document handling policies, an electronic record was maintained by State.[17] The consular officer who issued the visa said Shehhi probably was not interviewed, explaining that UAE nationals were not interviewed in connection with their visa applications unless   as did not happen in this case   there was a watchlist "hit."[18] UAE nationals were considered good visa risks both on economic and on security grounds.[19]

April 2000

April 2. **Nawaf al Hazmi's** visa expired,[20] but that expiration had no bearing on his legal status in the United States. Any visitor who enters the country with a valid visa may remain through the length of stay granted by an immigration inspector upon arrival.

April 5. Mihdhar and **Nawaf al Hazmi** acquired California driver's licenses.[21]

May 2000

May 17. **Mohammed Atta**, an Egyptian, applied for and on the next day received a five-year B-1/B-2 (tourist/business) visa from the U.S. embassy in Berlin, Germany.[22] The consular officer who adjudicated this visa said Atta "definitely" was not interviewed.

According to the officer, because he was a third-country national who had long been resident in Germany (approximately five years), the visa interview requirement was waived, and Atta was "basically treated like" a German citizen. German citizens do not need visas, as they participate in a "visa waiver" program. Another factor in his favor was Atta's strong record as a student in Germany.[23] Atta's visa application was destroyed prior to 9/11 pursuant to State Department policy then in effect, so we were able to review only the electronic record of his application.

Also on **May 17**, **Ramzi Binalshibh**, another Yemeni, applied for a B-1/B-2 (tourist/visa) visa in Berlin. He listed Agus Budiman in Washington, D.C., as the person he would be visiting in the United States. Although his application was denied, Binalshibh did not give up on trying to get a visa to the United States, as we will soon see.[24]

May 25. **Ziad Jarrah**, a native of Lebanon, applied for and received a five-year B-1/B-2 (tourist/business) visa in Berlin.[25] The consular officer who issued the visa could not recall whether he interviewed Jarrah. However, our review of Berlin visa policy for third-country nationals suggests that Jarrah was a strong visa candidate, given his long residence in Germany (approximately four years), academic involvement in Germany (at two universities), and Lebanese nationality. Third-country nationals with more than two years of residency in Germany met a threshold for visa approval. The officer who adjudicated his visa has stated that wealthy Lebanese families often sent their children to school in Germany as a way to keep them out of the Middle East's turmoil, and that Jarrah looked like one of those wealthy expatriates.[26]

May 29. Shehhi arrived in the United States for the first time from Brussels, Belgium, landing at Newark International Airport in New Jersey. He was admitted by immigration authorities as a tourist for six months. However, he was pulled aside by a "roving" Customs inspector who conducted a secondary inspection. He was admitted after this two-minute examination, during which his bags were x-rayed but he was not personally searched and was admitted. The Customs inspector was trained to look for drug couriers, not terrorists.[27]

June 2000

June 3. Atta arrived from Prague, Czech Republic, at Newark Airport as a tourist. He was given a customary six-month stay, valid until December 2, 2000.[28]

June 5. Binalshibh's May application was denied under INA section 221(g).[29] This section was routinely invoked by the U.S. embassy in Berlin, without conducting an interview, to deny a visa application that was incomplete or weak.[30] In such cases, the embassy would send a letter explaining the denial and inviting the submission of further documentation in support of the application.[31] Under the law, such additional information can become part of the original application.[32] The applicant then had six months to have the original denial reversed.[33]

June 10. Mihdhar left the United States against the wishes of the operational organizer of the plot, Khalid Sheikh Mohammed. He traveled to Yemen.[34]

June 15. **Binalshibh** attempted a second time to obtain a B-1/B-2 (tourist/business) visa in Berlin.

June 27. Jarrah entered the United States for the first time on a tourist visa.[35] He immediately violated his immigration status by going from the airport straight to full-time flight school. He studied at the Florida Flight Training Center in Venice, Florida, until January 31, 2001.[36] Jarrah never filed an application to change his status from tourist to student. This failure to maintain a legal immigration status provided a solid legal basis to deny him entry on each of the six subsequent occasions in which he reentered the United States. But because there was no student tracking system in place and because neither Jarrah nor the school complied with the law's notification requirements, immigration inspectors could not know he was out of status.

June 27. Binalshibh's second visa application was again denied under 221(g), apparently without his being interviewed by a consular officer.

July 2000

July 3. Shehhi and **Atta** enrolled at Huffman Aviation to take flight lessons.[37] Neither violated his immigration status: attending flight school was permitted as long as their entrance to the United States was legal and they sought to change their status before the expiration of their length of stay in late November and early December. As required by Huffman, both began training as private pilots.[38]

July 12. Nawaf al Hazmi filed to extend his stay in the United States, which was due to expire on July 14, 2000.[39] Yet another opportunity to spot the suspicious indicator of extremism in his passport.

July 18. A consular officer in Berlin interviewed **Binalshibh** in connection with his two visa applications submitted on May 17 and June 15, 2000. This time, a consular officer denied his application under INA Section 214(b), after concluding that Binalshibh had failed to prove that he was not an intending immigrant to the United States.[40] Under this provision, discussed more fully in Chapter 5, the nonimmigrant visa applicant bears the burden of establishing to the satisfaction of the consular officer that they are entitled to nonimmigrant status. The consular officer noted on the application that Binalshibh had a poor academic record at German universities, attending only sporadically. The officer also noted that Binalshibh had no apparent source of income, no apparent job, and was traveling back and forth to the Middle East. All these factors led the officer to consider Binalshibh a bad visa risk. There is no evidence that the officer denied Binalshibh because of concerns about terrorism.

August 2000

August 14. **Atta** and **Shehhi** passed their private pilot airplane test at Huffman Aviation. Atta received a score of 97 (out of 100) in 69 minutes. Shehhi received a score of 83 in 73 minutes.[41]

September 2000

September 3. **Ahmed al Ghamdi,** a Saudi, applied for and received a two-year B-1/B-2 (tourist/business) visa in Jeddah, Saudi Arabia. He presented a new Saudi passport only 13 days old. There is no evidence that he was interviewed.[42]

September 10. **Hani Hanjour** again applied for a B-1/B- (tourist/business) visa in Jeddah, Saudi Arabia, submitting a new passport issued on July 24, 2000. His statement on the application that he would like to stay for three years in the United States raised concerns among the consular staff that he was at risk of becoming an immigrant to the United States. A consular employee who screened Hanjour's application forwarded him to a consular officer for an interview. Hanjour told this officer that he was going to attend flight training school in the United States and wanted to change his status to "student" from "tourist" once he arrived in the United States.[43] "Look, you have spent enough time in the States" to know what you want to do there, the officer told Hanjour. His prior travel to the United States, the officer said to him, disqualified Hanjour from receiving a tourist visa in order to go to the United States and find a school "because he had been in the States long enough to decide what he wanted."[44] For these reasons, the officer denied Hanjour's application under INA section 221(g), a general denial that, as noted above, allowed the applicant to return with additional information in support of his application.

September 15. Huffman Aviation's Student Coordinator assisted **Atta** in filling out the student school form I-20M, required by the INS to demonstrate school enrollment.[45] **Shehhi** also received an I-20M signed by this coordinator. Both Atta's and Shehhi's I-539 applications to change their immigration status from tourist (B-1/B-2) to vocational student (M1) were mailed to the INS. Both applications requested that their status be maintained until September 1, 2001. The contents of the applications are substantially the same, including the same financial statement of support, bank statement, and lease.[46] Also in September, the two took flying lessons at Jones Aviation in nearby Sarasota, Florida. They spent a few hours a day flying at Jones, struggling as students because of their poor English. They were aggressive, even trying to take over control of the aircraft from the instructor on occasion. They failed their instrument rating tests there, and returned to Huffman.[47]

September 16. Binalshibh's third visa application was denied in Sanaa,Yemen, under INA section 214(b), the intending immigrant provision.[48] There is no evidence that concerns about terrorism played a role in this denial. The consular officer wrote on the application "no ties" and "previous refusals in Berlin."

September 19. Atta and **Shehhi's** I-539 applications were received by the INS.

September 25. **Hanjour** returned to the Jeddah consulate and, apparently having listened to what the consular officer told him, submitted another application for a student visa. This time, Hanjour stated a desire to attend the ELS Language Center in Oakland, California. A consular official   probably the intake screener   wrote a note on his application indicating that Hanjour had been denied a visa under section 221(g) on

September 10. The same consular officer who had interviewed Hanjour in connection with his September 10 application also processed this one. He recalled to us that Hanjour or someone acting on his behalf submitted an INS school enrollment form, or I-20 required to qualify for a student visa to the consulate late on September 25, 2000.[49] "It came to me, you know, at the end of the day to look at it. I saw he had an I-20, and it [his visa] was issued."[50]

State Department electronic records indicate that this approval allowed Hanjour to "overcome" his September 10 visa denial, another indication that multiple applications can be considered "one case." State Department records erroneously recorded the visa issued to Hanjour as a B-1/B-2 (business/tourist) visa when, in fact, it was an F (student) visa that was printed and put in Hanjour's passport.[51] In addition, Hanjour had already received an approved change of status to attend this same English language school in 1996. But that approval was granted by the INS in the United States, and the State Department had no record of it. The consular officer told us that if he had known this information, he might have refused Hanjour the visa.

October 2000

 October 17. **Hamza al Ghamdi**, a Saudi, applied for and received a two-year B-1/B-2 (tourist/business) visa in Riyadh, Saudi Arabia. His application was incomplete.[52] Al Ghamdi listed his occupation as "student" but left blank the question asking the street address of his school. Ghamdi's travel patterns indicated that he may have presented a passport containing fraudulent travel stamps associated with al Qaeda when he applied for this visa.[53] The consular officer who adjudicated his case was not familiar with this kind of manipulation; in addition, he told us that because of the workload in Jeddah, he rarely had time to thumb through passports. Ghamdi was not interviewed, because nothing in his application raised concerns in the mind of the consular officer who adjudicated it and there was no hit in the CLASS system.[54] His visa application was granted.

 October 23. **Mohand al Shehri**, a Saudi, applied for and received a two-year B-1/B-2 (tourist/business) visa in Riyadh, Saudi Arabia. His application was incomplete. Al Shehri listed his occupation as "student," but listed the street address of his school as "Riyadh K.S.A." He claimed he was a 21-year-old student who would be supporting himself in the United States.[55] He was not interviewed, according to the officer who issued this visa, because "We only interviewed Saudis if there was a previous denial of a visa application or if there was something wrong with the application."[56] Shehri apparently raised no such concerns. The officer noted that the lack of handwritten notes on the application was a further indication that he had not interviewed Shehri.[57]

October 25. **Binalshibh** applied for a visa again in Berlin, Germany, this time for a student (F) visa to attend aviation school in Florida. He accurately indicated on his application form that he had been denied visas previously in Berlin and Sanaa.

October 28. **Ahmed al Nami**, a Saudi, applied for and received a two-year B-1/B-2 (tourist/business) visa in Jeddah, Saudi Arabia. Nami's application was incomplete.[58] He listed his occupations as "student" but did not provide a complete address for his school. He listed his intending address in the United States as "in Los Angeles." Nami's passport may have contained fraudulent travel stamps associated with al Qaeda.[59] However, his passport did not survive, so we can not be sure. On his application, Nami indicated that "My friend Moshabab" would be traveling with him.

On the same day, **Mushabib al Hamlan**, a Saudi and a friend of 9/11 hijacker Ahmed al Nami, acquired a two-year B1/B2 (tourist/business) visa in Jeddah, Saudi Arabia.[60] Hamlan was selected to participate in the plot but backed out after obtaining his visa, perhaps at the urging of his family.

October 29. Jarrah arrived back in the United States, entering in Tampa, Florida, from Frankfurt, Germany, on a tourist visa. He received a six-month length of stay in the United States. He was still in flight school.[61]

November 2000

November 1. **Binalshibh** was denied in Berlin yet again under 221(g) for lack of adequate documentation and failure to show sufficient ties to Germany. His application was incomplete, and his prior denials in Berlin and Sanaa provided powerful grounds for this denial. Consular officials wrote on this application, "Incomplete [application], refused in Sanaa and here, bad case." Once again, there was no evidence that officials were concerned about terrorism. A citizen of a poor, developing country, with tenuous ties to Germany, Binalshibh was considered an intending immigrant and a bad visa risk.

November 6. Atta and **Shehhi** took their instrument rating airplane test at Huffman Aviation. Atta received a score of 90 in 122 minutes and Shehhi received a score of 75 in 89 minutes.[62] After passing this test, Atta and Shehhi were able to sign out planes. They did so on a number of occasions, often returning at 2:00 and 3:00 A.M. after logging four or five hours of flying time.[63]

November 12. **Ahmad al Haznawi,** a 20-year-old Saudi national, applied for and received a two-year B-1/B-2 (tourist/business) visa in Jeddah, Saudi Arabia.[64] There is evidence that Haznawi may have presented a passport with fraudulent travel stamps associated with al Qaeda.[65] Haznawi listed his occupation as "student" but left blank the line on which he was asked to supply the street address of his present school. He stated that he would provide financial support for his visit. He was not interviewed.

Also on **November 12**, **Saeed al Ghamdi**, a Saudi national, sometimes known as "Jihad" al Ghamdi   not to be confused with the 9/11 hijacker of the same name   applied for a B-1/B-2 (tourist/business) visa in Jeddah. Ghamdi's application was denied after he was interviewed by a consular officer who believed he was intending to immigrate to the United States. Ghamdi wrote on his application that he intended to stay in the United States for "12 months," a red flag because the usual period of admission for tourists granted by INS inspectors at ports of entry was six months. Contemporaneous notes by consular staff, probably taken during his interview, state: "To stay one year . . . no job . . .

graduated from H.S. last year . . . he has SR [Saudi rials] 10,000 only and staying one year! . . . Not working." Ghamdi was denied under INA section 214(b), the intending immigrant provision. There is no evidence that terrorism concerns played a role in this denial.[66]

November 20. **Majed Moqed,** a Saudi**,** applied for and received a two-year B-1/B-2 (tourist/business) visa in Riyadh, Saudi Arabia. His application was incomplete. He claimed to be a "student" but left blank the line on which he was asked to supply the street address of his present school.[67] The officer who adjudicated his visa said they did not interview Moqed: "I would have written some notes on the application form[] if I had."[68] He was not interviewed because, according to the officer who issued the visa, "We only interviewed Saudis if there was a previous denial of a visa application or if there was something wrong with the application."[69] Incompleteness by itself evidently did not trigger an interview.

November 21. **Satam al Suqami**, a Saudi**,** applied for and received a two-year B-1/B-2 (tourist/business) visa in Riyadh, Saudi Arabia.[70] There is very strong evidence that the passport Suqami submitted with this application had fraudulent travel stamps now associated with al Qaeda.[71] Suqami left blank the line on which he was asked to supply the name and street address of his present employer. The consular officer who issued the visa said he interviewed Suqami because he described his present occupation as "dealer," the word Saudis often put on their applications when they meant "businessman." The officer testified that he asked Suqami a number of questions, including, he believes, who was paying for the trip.[72] Although the officer stated that notes were always taken during interviews,[73] none were written on Suqami's application, raising the possibility that the officer's memory of having conducted an interview was false. In any case, Suqami evidently raised no suspicions and his application was approved.

November 25. Jarrah rented a private plane for a one-day trip from Miami to Nassau, Bahamas, with a couple of companions. There is no immigration departure record, but there is a record of his reentry into the country. At the general aviation terminal where Jarrah arrived, he was subjected to both an immigration and customs check, including an inspection of the plane by customs for the presence of drugs, contraband, and currency. Nothing unusual was found and Jarrah was once again admitted as a tourist for six months. Again, he was still in school despite having a B-1/B-2 visa.[74]

December 2000

December 8. Hanjour entered the United States for the final time at the Cincinnati/Northern Kentucky International Airport, six months after the entry of the other pilots. He never attended the ELS Language Center in Oakland, California, the stated destination on his second visa application of September 25, 2000. His records do not indicate the length of stay the primary immigration inspector gave him.[75]

December 12. **Zakariya Essabar**, a Moroccan who intended to participate in the plot, submitted the first of two visa applications in Berlin. He indicated that he intended to arrive in the United States on February 15, 2001.[76]

December 19. **Atta** and **Shehhi** took their commercial pilot license tests at Huffman Aviation, completing their schooling. Atta received a score of 93 in 116 minutes and Shehhi received a score of 73 in 99 minutes.[77]

2001

January 2001

January 4. Atta departed the United States for the first time, having overstayed his tourist visa by one month. Although his application for a change of his immigration status was still pending, once he departed the country the application was considered abandoned.[78]

January 5. Jarrah returned from Dusseldorf, Germany, landing at Newark, New Jersey, and flying onward to Tampa, Florida. He was admitted as a tourist for six months. His flight school education continued.[79]

January 10. **Essabar** was interviewed and was denied a visa under INA section 221(g), on the grounds that he provided no evidence of a job in or other ties to Germany. Essabar applied for a visa again on January 28, 2001, but there is no record of the State Department's ever having acted on this second application. On the same day, **Atta** returned from Madrid to Miami. The primary immigration inspector who screened him told the Commission that he had been working as a primary inspector for less than a year when Atta presented himself. He said he knew that if he took more time than 45 seconds to determine a visitor's admissibility or if he made too many referrals to secondary inspection, he could receive a poor performance appraisal. During an interview with the Department of Justice, Office of the Inspector General (DOJ OIG), in November 2001, the primary inspector recalled some of his encounter with Atta. He told the interviewer that Atta presented an Egyptian passport with a tourist/business visa and an INS student/school form indicating that he was attending school. The inspector determined that Atta needed either an F-1 visa to attend an academic school or an M-1 visa to attend a vocational school, and had neither. The official's "inspection results report" recorded Atta's statement that he had "turned in" a student/school form to the INS in an attempt to change his status, but that he "has not had a response [from the INS], meanwhile he's attending flight training school, already in school for 5/6 months."[80]
The inspector, however, had already begun to process Atta for admission into the United States before noticing the visa problem. The I-94 arrival record, which was stamped and stapled into Atta's passport, indicated that the primary inspector initially approved a one-month stay as a B-1 business visitor.[81]

The second red ink admission stamp (located on the top of Atta's passport in the figure) was that of a B-1 visitor, but the length of stay was left blank. We know this was the work of the primary inspector, as the stamp bears his assigned number. The inspector told us that the blank length of stay on the admission stamp indicated that while he was almost finished processing Atta, he stopped, realizing that Atta needed more scrutiny.[82] He sent him to a secondary immigration inspection for closer examination.

The immigration inspectors the Commission interviewed understood that INS policy permitted a commercial pilot coming to the United States for ongoing training to be admitted as a business visitor for the time necessary to complete his training. However, an alien wishing to pursue such training needed a vocational student visa.[83] The primary inspector initially thought that Atta was already a pilot who was seeking continuing education, and then decided that Atta was studying to become a pilot and had the wrong visa.

The ten-year veteran immigration inspector who conducted Atta's secondary examination admitted him as a tourist for eight months, though Atta had said he was still attending school and though as a tourist his stay should be legally limited to six months. This inspector initially recalled some aspects of this inspection in late 2001, when he was interviewed by the DOJ OIG; he said then that Atta was referred to secondary inspection as a possible overstay on a B1/B2 tourist visa. However, he told the Commission he no longer had any memory of this inspection and could not recall whether he asked Atta for his I-20 student/school form, checked the school/student system to verify Atta's information, or asked Atta whether he was a part-time or full-time student, was attending flight school, or was still in school. The same inspector told the DOJ OIG that he had checked INS computer databases for information on Atta and learned that the Egyptian had filed for a change of immigration status from tourist to student. He told the Commission that because the student tracking system at that time was "garbage"   full of information that was no longer valid and lacking updates   he would not have checked it to verify Atta's story that he was still in school.[84]

Yet the inspector told the DOJ OIG that he knew Atta had filed a change of immigration status from a computer check of his records. The inspector seems to have concluded that this application was still pending and that Atta was admissible. But under INS policy, Atta abandoned his application when he left the country. Other inspectors we interviewed were aware of this policy. Thus, Atta's entry into the United States with the wrong visa should have been grounds for his removal.[85]

The Commission sought to understand whether the secondary inspector's understanding of Atta's pending application affected the decision to admit him. In a subsequent 2002 interview with DOJ OIG, the inspector stated that if an alien departed the United States prior to his or her application for change of status being granted, then that application is considered abandoned. If that alien then seeks to reenter the United States as a student, he or she must obtain the correct student visa. Thus, according to the secondary inspector, Atta should not have been admitted. However, in response to a Commission staff question the inspector said that he thought the applicant in such a case "would still be in status; a gray area."[86]

In fact, this was not a gray area. Other inspectors we interviewed, including the primary inspector in this case, said that leaving the United States while an application for change of status was still pending made it necessary for the alien to get a new visa overseas. Indeed, the DOJ OIG concluded that the issue of the pending application was a red herring: all that mattered was whether Atta had the correct visa to enter the United States at the time he applied for entry.[87]

The secondary inspector admitted Atta as a B-2 tourist, which automatically set the length of stay at six months. Only a supervisor could vary this period, allowing a tourist to stay up to one year in the country. Every inspector we interviewed verified this. However, this inspector gave Atta eight months, until September 8, 2001, without supervisory approval. Thus, both Atta's admission as a tourist and his length of stay were improper.[88]

In addition, Atta had overstayed his previous visa by one month when he departed the United States on January 4, 2001.[89] That overstay should have been obvious to a secondary inspector tasked with giving a thorough look at Atta, for his passport would have contained an entry stamp into a foreign country from the week before, and an original U.S. admission stamp dated seven months earlier. Though the overstay did not make Atta automatically inadmissible, it could have been considered. But there is no indication that the secondary inspector who adjudicated Atta's admission took his overstay into account.[90] In contrast, other inspectors have told us that overstays are a typical travel pattern of an intending immigrant, and are normally a red flag for those attempting reentry.[91]

The secondary inspector also could have admitted Atta into the United States for 30 days for a fee of $170, requiring Atta to present paperwork from his school to prove his current student status within 30 days. However, the inspector told us he had not considered the option of a deferred inspection.[92] Such an inspection would have placed Atta in a difficult position: because he was already finished with school, he would have been unable to present paperwork indicating that he was still legally a student.

January 18. **Shehhi** arrived at JFK Airport in New York on Royal Moroccan Air from Casablanca.[93] He was screened by a ten-year veteran of immigration inspections at airports and the New York City seaport.[94] When Shehhi came up to the primary inspection counter, the "room was full, with numerous flights coming in at the same time." The inspector told the Commission that she was suspicious that Shehhi might be an intending immigrant, noting from the stamps in his passport that he had left the United States just a week earlier after a six-month stay. She typed into the computer record: "Sub left one week ago after entry in May. Has extension and now returning for a few more months." She referred Shehhi to a secondary immigration inspection for closer examination.[95]

The secondary inspector told the Commission that Shehhi wore conventional Western clothing, had glasses and facial hair, and "did not look like he had just come from boot camp." Though he had behaved badly in primary inspection, where his refusal to comply with the inspector's instruction to go to the secondary inspection room made an escort necessary, once there Shehhi waited until he was called and was not aggressive. About a dozen other visitors were called into secondary inspection in the ten minutes before Shehhi's referral.[96]

The secondary immigration inspector said that Shehhi had completed the required arrival and customs forms, adding that Shehhi spoke English well during the course of the 10 12 minute interview. "I had the impression Shehhi had money," the inspector said. "I remember looking at his passport, and it showed he had been in and out of the United States and there were other travel stamps. I remember asking how much money he had he had a substantial amount, three credit cards and more than $2,000."[97]

Shehhi also mentioned applying for an extension of stay in the United States to remain until September 8, 2001; after waiting months for an answer and not getting one, he had finally left. To the inspector, "that seemed reasonable." The inspector told the Commission he was not aware that leaving the country while an immigration benefit application was pending amounted to abandoning that application.[98]

The inspector asked Shehhi the purpose of his trip to the United States, trying to determine if he intended to remain permanently, as the primary inspector suspected. Shehhi told the inspector that he was coming back to the United States for continued flight training, that he had previously attended Huffman Aviation School, and that he was finished with flight school but wanted to log more hours in the sky. The inspector thought Shehhi was seeking private flying lessons, but did not ask Shehhi for supporting documentation.[99]

The inspector did not recall whether Shehhi showed him any papers to verify his previous flight school attendance at Huffman Aviation, nor whether he had asked for such paperwork. "I didn't have any doubt he did go to school, and I didn't think he was trying to use his change of status application to remain here in the United States for illegitimate reasons. My belief was that he was coming back to log flight hours with a private instructor." Under this inspector's understanding of INS guidelines, a pilot here for a form of continuing education, such as private flight lessons, may be admitted as a business visitor. Although the baseline time at JFK International for business visitors was three months, Shehhi asked for four and got it.[100]

The inspection results tell a somewhat different story; they read: "Was in U.S. gaining flight hours to become a pilot. Admitted for four months." They thus suggest that the inspector actually may have considered Shehhi a student, not already a pilot.

The difference between Shehhi being a student seeking to become a pilot or already was a pilot was not an insignificant nuance. According to immigration law applied at ports of entry, if Shehhi was already a pilot, the B-1 business entry he was granted was arguably legitimate. However, if Shehhi was a full-time student, his admission as a business visitor was erroneous. And because Shehhi, like Atta, had left the country while his application for a change of immigration status was still pending, this application should have been considered "abandoned." In other words, Shehhi needed to obtain the proper student visa overseas in order to reenter the United States. The facts of this adjudication are simply not clear enough to reach a conclusion about the appropriateness of this entry.

January 26. Jarrah departed the United States for the fourth time.[101]

February 2001

February 25. Jarrah enters for the fifth time at Newark as a business visitor, but still receives a six-month stay. This was unusual, as most inspectors told us that standard operating procedures were to give business visitors a stay of one or three months, depending on the port, and six months only when the visitor could document the purpose of the stay.[102]

March 2001

March 30. Jarrah departed for the fifth time.[103]

April 2001

April 12. Shehhi obtained a Florida driver's license.[104]

April 13. Jarrah entered at Atlanta from Amsterdam and was granted a three and a half month stay on business.[105]

April 21. **Ahmed al Nami** acquired a new Saudi passport, #C505363, replacing the one (#C115007) he had used to acquire a visa on October 28, 2000, in Jeddah, a visa he never used. He may have acquired this new passport because there was evidence of travel to Afghanistan in his previous one.[106]

April 23. Nami applied for and received a B-1/B-2 (tourist/business) visa in Jeddah with his new passport. There is evidence from a handwritten note on his application that Nami was interviewed briefly, either by a consular officer or by a consular staff member, to clarify an entry on his application. The words "My friend Mosh" are crossed out under the question asking the "names and relationships of people traveling with you." This is probably a reference to Mushabib al Hamlan, another potential 9/11 hijacker who applied for a visa with Nami on October 28, 2000. Nami also crossed out a box checked "no" under the question asking if he had ever applied for a U.S. visa previously, changing his answer to "yes." It is not clear what prompted this change — possibly his brief interaction with a consular official — but it is accurate. However, he failed to complete his response and state where and when he had previously applied for a U.S. visa. Doing so would have revealed that he was applying for a new visa long before the expiration of the two-year visa he acquired the previous October. Nami's action could have raised questions, had it been coupled with the fact that he was applying with a new passport. But it would not have been noticed by the consular officer who issued the visa, because Saudis were not required to fill in their applications fully, Saudis were rarely interviewed, and State's name check system did not automatically call up prior visa issuances; it called up only prior refusals.[107]

April 23. Waleed al Shehri and **Satam al Suqami**, both Saudis, entered together at Orlando from Dubai, United Arab Emirates. Suqami was the only Saudi muscle hijacker admitted on business, and only for one month. Shehri was admitted as a tourist for a six-month stay. Both were admitted by the same primary immigration inspector.[108] Suqami's passport survived the attack: a passerby picked it up from the World Trade Center and handed to a New York Police Department detective shortly before the towers collapsed.[109] Later analysis showed that it contained what are now believed to be fraudulent travel stamps associated with al Qaeda.[110] Upon reviewing color copies of the document, the inspector who admitted Suqami told the Commission he did not note any such fraud.[111] Indeed, he could not have been expected to identify the fraud at the time of Suqami's admission — it was not discovered by the intelligence community until after the attacks.

May 2001

May 2. **Majed Moqed** and **Ahmed al Ghamdi** arrived together at Dulles International Airport in Washington, D.C. Both Saudis were admitted as tourists for six months by different immigration inspectors. Ghamdi's Customs declaration indicated that he had more than $10,000 with him upon entry, but the Customs inspector who processed him did not fill out the required additional electronic forms when money in excess of $10,000 is brought into the United States.[112]

Also on this day, **Shehhi** arrived in Miami and was granted a six-month tourist stay.[113] Meanwhile, **Atta** and, we believe, **Jarrah** were attempting to extend Jarrah's length of stay to September 2001.

Atta's walk-in inspection at the Miami Immigration District Office

On May 2, 2001, Atta and two companions stood in a long line at the Miami District Immigration Office. INS district offices adjudicate all types of immigration benefits inspections, including naturalization interviews, applications for permanent residency based on marriage to a U.S. citizen, and deferred inspections for students lacking the proper paperwork upon entry. But Atta had something else in mind. He wanted his companion, who was likely Jarrah, to obtain the same eight-month length of stay that he had (wrongfully) received in January.[114]

By late morning, Atta finally made it to the inspection desk. An inspector from Miami International Airport was getting ready to take a break for lunch at about 11:30 A.M. when three men approached her at the counter. This inspector had worked primary and secondary inspections at airports, as well as of ship crews, since 1988 in Fort Lauderdale and Miami. However, because she had never before worked at this district office, she recalled the encounter with Atta vividly.[115]

One of Atta's companions, proficient in English, spoke first. He told the inspector, "My friends have a question about their I-94 arrival records." When she asked, "Do you need to see immigration?" he said no. The inspector then instructed him to go sit down and that she would help him with his friends, and he complied. She told them that the person needing help should write his name on the sign-in sheet. In large capital letters, he wrote, "ATTA."[116]

Atta told the inspector that he wanted his friend to receive an eight-month length of stay as he had. The inspector recalled taking both passports to see if they had genuine visas. She also looked at the I-94 arrival records in the passports. Atta's companion had received a six-month stay as a tourist, with an end date of September 8, 2001. She also noticed that Atta had been admitted as a tourist for eight months. During this time, Atta was quiet. She told Atta, "Someone gave you the wrong admission and I'm not giving your friend eight months."[117]

The inspector then went to her supervisor, informed him that Atta had been granted an incorrect length of stay, and asked permission to roll it back to six months. The supervisor agreed. The inspector then tore the I-94 record out of Atta's passport, and created a new I-94 for six months, which allowed Atta to remain in the United States until July 9, 2001. On the record she wrote: "I-94 issued in error at MIA [Miami International Airport]. New I-94 issued." The inspector then took a red-inked admission stamp, rolled the date back to January 10, and stamped Atta as a B-2 tourist. She wrote in a length of stay until July 9, 2001, and handed Atta back his passport and new I-94 record. Atta took the documents, said thank you, and left with his companions.[118]

May 2. Atta and **Jarrah** acquired Florida driver's licenses.[119]

May 4. Waleed al Shehri obtained a Florida driver's license.[120]

May 5. Waleed al Shehri acquired a duplicate Florida driver's license, this time with a different address.[121]

May 16. **Waleed al Shehri** and **Suqami** again traveled together, this time out of the country to the Bahamas, where they reserved three nights at the Bahamas Princess Resort.[122] They turned in their arrival record, which was now acting as an exit record, boarded the plane, and arrived in Freeport.[123] The trip was intended to extend Suqami's legal length of stay in the United States.[124] Bahamian immigration refused the two entry, however, because neither had a Bahamian visa.[125] They therefore had to return to their starting point, in this case Fort Lauderdale. Because they never entered the Bahamas, under U.S. immigration law they had never left the United States. After being refused entry by the Bahamian INS at Freeport, they were sent through U.S. "pre-clearance" before boarding the plane back to Miami. By making possible immigration inspections of U.S.-bound travelers prior to their arrival, preclearance helped ease the burden of admission at busy U.S. airports. These stations also prevented travelers deemed inadmissible from boarding U.S.-bound planes.[126] In this preclearance process, immigration waived them through but customs stopped Shehri. The inspection lasted one minute; Shehri was not personally searched, nor was his luggage x-rayed. They boarded a plane and returned to Miami.[127]

May 20. Suqami joined the millions of overstays in the United States after failing to file for an extension of stay with the INS after he returned from the Bahamas. Had he been allowed into the Bahamas, upon his return to the United States he would have likely been granted an additional length of stay in the country as a tourist. As it was, he remained in illegal status until September 11.

May 24. Jarrah obtained a duplicate Florida driver's license.[128]

May 28. **Hamza al Ghamdi, Mohand al Shehri**, and **Ahmed al Nami** arrived together at Miami from Dubai, United Arab Emirates.[129] The three Saudis were admitted as tourists for six months by different primary inspectors.[130]

June 2001

June 1. The Visa Express Program was introduced for all Saudi citizens applying for visas in Saudi Arabia in an effort to make the consular workload more manageable and to reduce the size of the crowds outside of the embassy. The concept was simple. Instead of going to the U.S. consulate to apply for a visa, the applicant filled out the form at one of ten approved travel agencies. After collecting the application, the visa application fee, and the applicant's passport, the travel agency delivered these documents to the embassy in Riyadh or to the consulate in Jeddah, and picked up the package of documents the next day. If the application was approved, then the agency was responsible for returning the passport (now containing the visa) to the applicant. If the consular officials determined that an interview was necessary, then the travel agency was responsible for so notifying the applicant by providing him or her with a letter from the consular section. Applicants were rejected only after an in-person interview.[131] (Visa Express will be discussed in further detail in chapter 5.)

June 8. **Ahmad al Haznawi** and **Wail al Shehri** arrived together at Miami from Dubai, United Arab Emirates. Both Saudis were admitted as tourists for six months by the same primary inspector.[132]

June 10. **Saeed al Ghamdi** acquired a new Saudi passport, #C573895, replacing the one (#B516222) he used to acquire a visa on September 4, 2000, in Jeddah. He may have acquired this new passport because there was evidence of travel to Afghanistan in his previous passport.[133]

June 12. Just like Nami (who applied April 23), **Saeed al Ghamdi** acquired a second two-year B-1/B-2 (tourist/business) visa in Jeddah. His application was incomplete and he was not interviewed. Ghamdi's visa application indicated that he had never applied for a U.S. visa before, a curious similarity to Nami's application.[134] This was not true, since he had applied for and acquired a visa on September 4, 2000. However, the State Department computer system was not set up to catch this false statement; as noted above, it called up only prior refusals. Ghamdi's application was submitted by Minhal Travel and processed through the Visa Express program.[135] We considered the possibility that the false answer reflected a mistake by the travel agency personnel, but the same signature appears on both visa applications, and State records indicate that the September application was submitted in person. Thus, it appears that Ghamdi was directly involved in preparing the June visa application containing the false statement. He may have omitted information about his prior visa in order not to raise suspicion about his new visa application in his new passport   without the travel to Pakistan and Afghanistan   when his old visa, which was multiple entry, was still valid.

June 13. **Mihdhar** applied for and received his second B-1/B-2 (tourist/business) visa in Jeddah. Mihdhar's passport had been issued only 13 days earlier and, like up two other hijackers, it contained an indicator of possible terrorist affiliation   still unknown at that time to U.S. intelligence officials. His application was incomplete. For example, he listed his occupation as "businessman," but left blank the name and street address of his present employer. Mihdhar's application also indicated that he had not previously applied for a U.S. visa or been to the United States, though he had in fact traveled to the United States on a B-1/B-2 visa issued in April 1999 (also in Jeddah). Thus, his application contained two false statements. However, the State Department's computer system was not set up to catch these false statements by bringing up Mihdhar's prior visa history. Mihdhar's application was processed through the Visa Express program, and his application was submitted by Al Tayyar Travel. It is possible that these questions were answered falsely because of a mistake by the travel agency personnel; and unlike Ghamdi's, Mihdhar's application was signed only on the line for the "preparer" of the application. It is unclear why Mihdhar or the travel agency would wish to hide the fact of his prior travel. Mihdhar may have feared that it could compromise operational security of the 9/11 plot. He also may not have wanted to highlight that he had obtained a new passport since his previous visa.[136]

Consular officials have told us that evidence of the prior visas or travel to the United States actually would have reduced concern that the applicants were intending to immigrate. Thus, if the officers had learned the truth about these issues   and received an adequate explanation for the mistakes on the applications   they likely would have had no good reason to deny visas to these hijackers. On the other hand, if they had interviewed Mihdhar, Nami, and Ghamdi and received suspicious answers to their questions, the outcome might well have been different.

June 18. The INS belatedly approved **Nawaf al Hazmi's** extension of stay to January 15, 2001. Technically, the application was late, since the INS received it in July 2000, after his length of stay had expired; they therefore should not have adjudicated it. However, even with this late adjudication Hazmi was still an overstay as of January 16, 2001. Hazmi never knew that his extension had been approved   the notice was returned as "undeliverable" on March 25, 2002.

June 18. **Abdul Aziz al Omari,** a Saudi, applied for and received a two-year B-1/B-2 (tourist/business) visa in Jeddah, Saudi Arabia. There is strong evidence that Omari presented a passport containing the travel stamps now known to be associated with al Qaeda when he applied for this visa since the fraudulent stamps predate this application. Moreover, his application was incomplete, and he listed his home address as a hotel in Jeddah. He was not interviewed. His application was processed through the Visa Express program and was submitted by Attar Travel.[137]

June 18. **Fayez Banihammad,** an Emirati, applied for and received a B-1/B-2 (tourist/business) visa in Abu Dhabi, United Arab Emirates. Banihammad's passport was only five days old. His application was incomplete; a number of sections were left completely blank.[138] The consular officer who adjudicated this visa has stated that interviews were almost never required of UAE nationals in connection with their visa applications, that the UAE was considered a welfare state that took very good care of its citizens, and that the UAE was treated as a de facto visa waiver country.[139] Banihammad, a former immigration officer in the UAE, was not interviewed.[140]

June 19. Marwan al Shehhi acquired a duplicate Florida driver's license.[141]

June 20. **Salem al Hazmi,** a Saudi, applied for and received a two-year B-1/B-2 (tourist/business) visa in Jeddah, Saudi Arabia. His application was incomplete, and he listed his occupation as "unemployed." The passport he supplied was four days old and contained an indicator of possible terrorist affiliation.[142] His application, processed through the Visa Express program, was submitted by Ace Travel. According to the consular officer who approved this application, the fact that Hazmi was "unemployed" was not of concern "because they have a terrible unemployment problem in Saudi Arabia, and a lot of people have money but they don't have jobs."[143] Although unemployment would have been a "big deal" in another country, the officer said, Saudis like Hazmi "weren't looking for jobs even though they were unemployed."[144]

June 25. Nawaf al Hazmi obtained a Florida driver's license.[145]

June 26. Hamza al Ghamdi obtained a Florida identification card.[146]

June 27. Banihammad and **Saeed al Ghamdi** arrived at Orlando from Dubai. The two were processed by different primary inspectors. Banihammad was admitted as a tourist for six months.[147] Although he handed in customs and immigration forms using two different names, the anomaly was not noted, because customs and INS inspectors did not review each other's forms. The immigration inspector who admitted Banihammad told the Commission that in the 45 seconds allowed for processing each visitor, it was not possible to fully check the contents of the forms. He said that if he had noticed the two different names forms he would have referred Banihammad to a secondary inspection, suspecting that the Emirati was attempting to hide his true identity.[148]

Saeed al Ghamdi, a Saudi, was admitted as a tourist for six months, but only after a secondary inspection. The Orlando primary inspector who referred him for further examination had worked as an immigration inspector for three years. He said that he insisted that a visitor communicate with him in order to be admitted and that he always asked to see a return ticket. The inspector also told us that he looked closely to see whether the Customs declaration and I-94 arrival form listed a full address of intended destination. Ghamdi met none of these requirements.[149]

Saeed al Ghamdi's June 27, 2001 Customs declaration reviewed by the primary inspector during his adjudication.

The inspector's inspection record reads, "Subject speaks very little English. No return ticket, no address listed; please question."[150] His Customs declaration, listing $500 for a stay of one month, was, according to the primary inspector, "pushing it a little bit, along with the fact that he didn't know where he was going." The inspector confirmed that he did not have the discretion to give Ghamdi the one-month stay he sought   the law required a mandatory six-month stay for tourists traveling on a visa. The inspector referred Ghamdi to secondary inspection so an interpreter could attempt to flesh out his purpose in coming to the United States.[151]

In secondary inspection, Ghamdi convinced a different inspector that he was a tourist and admissible. His secondary inspection report reads: "Tourist. Valid docs. Sufficiently financed. B-2, six months." Although the inspector who admitted Ghamdi does not recall the inspection, which lasted ten minutes, he told the Commission that he did not normally consider money a valid criterion for determining admissibility. He told us that Ghamdi must have had credit cards to supplement the $500 in cash he was carrying. The inspector said he was not concerned that Ghamdi's arrival record failed to list an exact address; central Florida is overflowing with hotel rooms and thus a tourist need not have precise lodging to be admissible. Ghamdi's travel documents looked valid to him as well.[152]

June 29. Abdul Aziz al Omari and **Salem al Hazmi** arrived at JFK Airport in New York from Dubai, United Arab Emirates. Both Saudis were admitted as tourists for six months by the same immigration inspector.[153] Omari's passport was doctored, containing what we believe are the same fraudulent travel stamps associated with al Qaeda.[154] The passport survived the attacks on the World Trade Center because Omari's luggage never made it onto the plane when he transferred from his flight from Portland, Maine. Salem al Hazmi's passport contained an indicator of possible terrorist affiliation. We know this because a digital image of Hazmi's passport was found on a hard drive in a safehouse in Pakistan.[155]

Ahmed al Nami obtained a Florida state identification card.[156]

July 2001

July 2. Hamza al Ghamdi obtained a Florida driver's license; **Mohand al Shehri,** a Florida identification card. **Moqed** and **Salem al Hazmi** acquired USA identification cards in July.[157] The Hazmi brothers' identifications were found in the rubble at the Pentagon and appeared genuine upon examination.[158]

July 3. **Wail al Shehri** acquired a Florida identification card.[159]

July 4. **Mihdhar** reentered the United States at JFK Airport.[160] He was on no watchlist, though he should have been watchlisted in January 2000. He was admitted as a business visitor for three months   the standard at JFK for a business entry.[161] His passport contained an indicator or possible terrorist affiliation. [162] Two and a half years later, the inspector who admitted Mihdhar on July 4, 2001, still could not identify the indicator, as the information has yet to be unclassified and disseminated to the field. She did note, however, that Mihdhar's passport, which had been acquired a month earlier, lacked an expiration date; that absence, she told us, could have been a bar to admission had it been noticed.[163]

July 4. **Mohamed al Kahtani,** a Saudi**,** applied for and received a two-year B-1/B-2 (tourist/business) visa in Riyadh, Saudi Arabia. He was processed through Visa Express. There is no evidence that Kahtani was interviewed.[164]

July 5. In the West Wing, the Counterterrorism Security Group of the NSC, headed by Richard Clarke, hosted an emergency CIA briefing for operational agencies, including INS, Customs, U.S. Secret Service, FBI, FAA, and Coast Guard. The INS and Customs sent two people each to the briefing; none were senior managers. Only one of them had heard any threat reporting on al Qaeda prior to this meeting. The attendees said the briefer told them that there was to be no dissemination of the information discussed at the meeting. The discussion focused on the potential of an overseas target, but a domestic attack was not ruled out.[165] An NSC official recalls a somewhat different emphasis, saying that attendees were asked ti take the information back to their home agencies and "do what you can" with it, subject to classification and distribution restrictions.

The midlevel INS intelligence analyst who attended the meeting, who had never been to the White House before, recalled in her interview with us that during the meeting the briefer discussed the possibility of "Mideastern" terrorists attempting entry into the United States using European passports. This same analyst summarized the meeting in a report, briefed her boss, and called the White House after the meeting to request declassification of the information so that she might develop a threat advisory for the ports of entry. She never received a response. Nor did the acting commissioner of the INS at the time, Kevin Rooney, ever hear about the meeting or a potential threat from al Qaeda. However, the Customs attendee at the meeting, somewhat familiar with the atmosphere of threat at this time, decided that the information was important to get to all inspectors in the field through the shared customs and INS computer system, TECS, and prepared a "Terrorism Advisory   Heightened Threat Environment."[166]

July 6. The threat advisory compiled by the Customs officer contained unclassified information that supported the classified information briefed by the CIA the previous day. The message was received by all immigration and customs personnel at ports of entry, but was addressed only to Customs employees. It did not contain any operational information about persons, places, or travel documents. The alert listed five ongoing U.S. trials of radical Islamic terrorists and warned:

> U.S. Customs personnel are requested to be vigilant during the summer months against potential threats from foreign terrorists against U.S. interests domestically and abroad. Recent terrorist trials and convictions (noted below) have created an environment of heightened animosity towards the U.S. from extremists looking for an opportunity to attack. If you encounter suspicious activity suggesting a potential terrorist attack follow your established security procedures, coordinate with the local office of Investigations and advise Headquarters, Anti-Terrorism Intelligence Section.[167]

July 7. **Atta** departed the country, as the abbreviated length of stay he received from the Miami District Office inspector expired on July 9.[168]

July 10. Haznawi obtained a Florida driver's license with a learner's permit. **Jarrah** acquired a duplicate Florida driver's license.[169] **Saeed al Ghamdi** and **Banihammad** got Florida state identification cards. **Mihdhar, Nawaf al Hazmi,** and **Omari** acquired USA identification cards.[170]

July 17. Atta's application to change his immigration status from tourist to student was approved to September 1, 2001. The application was approved by the same person who adjudicated Shehhi's change of status application in September 2000.[171]

July 19. **Atta** entered the United States for the last time, returning from Madrid on July 19 at Hartsfield Atlanta International Airport. Atta was admitted as a business visitor until November 12, 2001.[172] The primary inspector who screened him did not recall the entry.[173] Because Atta had only been out of the United States for three weeks during the previous 13 months, he should have been flagged as an intending immigrant and was a candidate for a secondary inspection. There was no secondary inspection, however, and Atta was now legally in the United States until the day of the planned attack.

July 23. **Khalid Sheikh Mohamed (KSM)**, a Pakistani and the chief tactical planner and coordinator of the 9/11 attacks, obtained a B-1/B-2 (tourist/business) visa to visit the United States.[174] Although he was not a Saudi citizen and we do not believe he was in Saudi Arabia at the time, he applied for a visa using a Saudi passport under the alias of "Abdulrahman al Ghamdi." On his application, KSM listed his address in the United States as "New York." We believe someone else submitted his application, passport, and a photo to the U.S. embassy in Riyadh through the Visa Express program from the travel agency Minhal Travel,[175] the same agency used by Saeed al Ghamdi for his June 12 application.[176] Because he used an alias, KSM obtained a visa even though he was on the TIPOFF terrorist watchlist since 1996. There is no evidence that KSM ever used this visa under this alias to enter the United States.

Acquisition of Virginia identification cards. Three Salvadoran immigrants living in Virginia, two illegally and one as a lawful permanent resident, were found guilty of helping four September 11 operatives use fraudulent documentation to obtain Virginia identification documents. Two were convicted of helping **Ahmed al Ghamdi** and **Abdul Aziz al Omari** obtain fraudulent residency certificates.[177] Another was convicted of providing false residency information on behalf of **Hanjour** and **Mihdhar** after being solicited by the two hijackers at a 7-Eleven in Falls Church, Virginia. For a fee, the Salvadoran falsely certified his old Virginia address as the residence of the hijackers.[178] These residency certificates were then used to support their applications for Virginia identification cards issued by the Department of Motor Vehicles on August 1 and 2, 2001, respectively.[179] The Salvadoran's address was also recycled by **Moqed** and **Salem al Hazmi** to use on their Virginia identification cards issued on August 2, 2001.[180] **Jarrah** followed suit on August 29, using a fictitious residency address and a certification of that address by Hanjour, who again used the address provided to him on August 1, 2001 to acquire his Virginia identification card.[181] One of the men charged in these cases recognized these hijackers as having been together at the Arlington, Virginia, DMV on August 2, 2001.[182] In all, the five hijackers based their Virginia identification documents on the residency information of one bribed Salvadoran.

August 2001

August 1. Mihdhar and **Hanjour** fraudulently obtained Virginia identification cards in Falls Church. **Ahmed al Ghamdi** and **Moqed** obtained USA identification cards in August as well.[183]

August 2. Ahmed al Ghamdi, Moqed, Salem al Hazmi, and **Omari** acquired Virginia identification cards, with help of Mihdhar and Hanjour. All of these identifications were obtained fraudulently.

August 4. Mohamed al Kahtani, a Saudi, the only operative other than Mihdhar who appears to have attempted a solo entry, arrived on August 4, 2001 at Orlando, Florida. He was also the only operative to be refused entry to the United States.[184] Records indicate that Atta was waiting for him at Orlando International while Kahtani was in secondary immigration inspection. Atta did not leave the Orlando airport until after it was clear that Kahtani was going back home.[185]

Both the primary and secondary inspectors remembered Kahtani well. Records indicate that Kahtani presented a Saudi passport with a two-year U.S. tourist visa. The primary inspector said that she recalled Kahtani for two reasons: he was the first Saudi she had ever encountered in her four years at Orlando that claimed to not speak English and his customs and arrival forms were not filled out. More subjectively, he made the inspector feel uneasy. Because she was unable to adequately communicate with Kahtani, she referred him to secondary inspection.[186] The secondary inspector who refused to admit Kahtani into the United States testified before the Commission on January 26, 2004.[187]

The secondary inspector who recommended and gained approval from his supervisor to deny Kahtani entry developed his interviewing skills as a 26-year veteran of the U.S. Army, through limited INS training, and ten years of experience conducting primary and secondary inspections at Miami and Orlando airports. The inspector noted Kahtani's hostility from the moment he called his name through the hour and a half spent interviewing him with the help of a Department of Justice translator. Kahtani was clean-cut with a military build. He had no return ticket and became threatening when asked where he was going, how long he was going to stay, and who was meeting him. Although he had enough cash for a ticket home, he did not have any credit cards.

Kahtani's answers to questions kept changing. Without a return ticket and limited funds, the secondary inspector sought to exclude him as an intending immigrant. The inspector's real concern, however, was that Kahtani was up to no good. The inspector told the Commission in his written testimony:

> My first question to the subject (through the interpreter) was why he was not in possession of a return airline ticket. The subject became visibly upset and in an arrogant and threatening manner, which included pointing his finger at my face, stated that he did not know where he was going when he departed the United States. What first came to mind at this point was that this subject was a "hit man." When I was in the Recruiting Command, we received extensive training in questioning techniques. A "hit man" doesn't know where he is going because if he is caught, that way he doesn't have any information to bargain with.[188]

This inspector had noted on prior occasions that Saudis coming through Orlando had a reputation for spending a lot of money at Disney World. Denying a Saudi entry was unusual, and inspectors told us they were generally concerned about the repercussions of taking such a step. However, after Kahtani refused to answer any questions under oath, the inspector decided to seek his supervisor's approval to recommend that Kahtani be barred as an "expedited removal," meaning that he could be deported without a hearing. After the inspector was questioned, approval to remove Kahtani was granted. The inspector convinced Kahtani to pay his own way home, saving paperwork and government funds.[189]

Because an "adverse action" was taken against Kahtani, he was required to be digitally photographed and fingerprinted through the INS biometric system. (This action would help to quickly verify Kahtani's identity when he was detained in Afghanistan after 9/11.) His passport was copied, although the inspector noted no fraudulent manipulations. In fact, Kahtani's passport does contain a stamp listed as fraudulent and associated with al Qaeda.[190] The inspector did not check Kahtani's luggage.

August 9. Shehhi's application to change his immigration status from tourist to student was approved through September 1, 2001.

August 23. The CIA sent a classified electronic message to the State Department, FBI, INS and the Customs Service, recommending that **Mihdhar** and **Hazmi** be added to the watchlist database accessible to the INS and Customs. They were suspected terrorists.[191]

August 24. Both **Hazmi** and **Mihdhar** were entered into separate lookouts. These lookouts are automatically checked when passports are scanned at ports of entry. The lookouts were identical, warning of "possible travel to the U.S." Immigration inspectors were instructed to refer them to secondary immigration inspection and to notify investigations and intelligence divisions at headquarters if they attempted to enter the United States. In addition, their passport numbers and travel itinerary were to be recorded.[192] These lookouts were not used by U.S. airlines to screen passengers seeking to fly on domestic flights.

August 27. **Ali Abdul Aziz Ali**, the nephew of Khalid Sheikh Mohammed, applied for a U.S. visa in Dubai, United Arab Emirates. Ali's application stated that he intended to enter the United States on September 4, 2001, for "one week." As a Pakistani visa applicant in a third country, he would have received close scrutiny from U.S. officials. In any event, it was deemed possible that he intended to immigrate, and accordingly he was denied a visa under section 214(b).[193]

August 27. Hamza al Ghamdi acquired a duplicate Florida driver's license.[194]

August 29. Jarrah obtained a Virginia identification card, with the help of Hanjour and Mihdhar.[195]

August 31. A new listing for **Mihdhar** was placed in an INS and Customs lookout database, describing him as "armed and dangerous" and someone who must be referred to secondary inspection.[196]

Identification Documents of the 9/11 Hijackers

Mohamed Atta FL DL, 05/02/01	Marwan al Shehhi FL DL, 04/12/01 FL DL duplicate, 6/19/01
Khalid al Mihdhar CA DL, 04/05/00 USA ID card, 07/10/01 VA ID card, 08/01/01	Nawaf al Hazmi CA DL, 04/05/00 FL DL, 06/25/01 USA ID card, 07/10/01 VA ID card, 08/02/01

Hani Hanjour AZ DL, 11/29/91 FL ID card, 04/15/96 VA ID card, 08/01/01 Failed VA DL test, 08/02/01 MD ID card, 09/05/01	Ziad Jarrah FL DL, 05/02/01 FL DL duplicate 5/24/01 VA ID card, 08/29/01
Satam al Suqami No DL or ID card	Waleed al Shehri FL DL, 05/04/01 (duplicate issued with different address, 05/05/01)
Ahmed al Ghamdi USA ID card, 07/2001 VA ID card, 08/02/2001	Majed Moqed USA ID card, 07/2001 VA ID card, 08/02/2001
Hamza al Ghamdi FL ID card, 06/26/01 FL DL, 07/02/01 (duplicate issued 08/27/01)	Mohand al Shehri FL ID card, 07/02/01
Ahmed al Nami FL DL, 06/29/01	Wail al Shehri FL DL, 07/03/01
Ahmed al Haznawi FL DL, 07/10/00 (duplicate issued 09/07/01)	Fayez Banihammad FL ID, 07/10/01
Saeed al Ghamdi FL ID card, 07/10/01	Salem al Hazmi USA ID card, 07/01/01[197] VA ID card, 08/02/01
Abdul Aziz al Omari USA ID card, 07/10/2001 VA ID card, 08/02/2001	

September 2001

September 4. The State Department used its visa revocation authority under section 221(i) of the Immigration and Nationality Act to revoke **Mihdhar's** visa under section 212(A)(3)(b) of the Immigration and Nationality Act for his participation in terrorist activities.[198]

September 5. **Hanjour** obtained a Maryland identification card.[199]

The same day, the INS entered the September 4 notice of revocation of Mihdhar's visa into the INS lookout system. State identified Mihdhar as a potential witness in an FBI investigation, and inspectors were told not to detain him.[200]

September 7. Brothers **Salem** and **Nawaf al Hazmi**, along with **Moqed**, requested that their Virginia identification cards be reissued. **Haznawi** obtained a duplicate Florida driver's license.[201]

September 11. As the hijackers boarded four flights, American Airlines Flights 11 and 77, and United Airlines Flights 93 and 175, at least six used U.S. identification documents acquired in the previous months, three of which were fraudulently obtained in northern Virginia.[202] Suqami, the only hijacker who did not have a state-issued identification, used his Saudi passport as check-in identification for American Airlines Flight 11.[203]

Findings of Fact - Visas

When we examine the outcomes of the 9/11 conspirators' engagement with the visa issuance process, we see they are consistent with a system focused on excluding intending immigrants and dependent on a name check of a database to search for criminals and terrorists. When hijackers or conspirators appeared to be intending immigrants, as happened most often when applicants were from poorer countries, they were denied a visa. If they met that threshold, however, and the name check came up clean, there was little to prevent them from entering the United States. Among our findings:

- Fourteen of the 19 September 11 hijackers obtained new passports shortly before they applied for their U.S. visas.

- Three of the hijackers, Khalid al Mihdhar, Nawaf al Hazmi, and Salem al Hazmi, presented with their visa applications passports that contained an indicator of possible terrorist affiliation. We know now that Mihdhar and Salem al Hazmi each possessed at least two passports, all with this indicator.

- There is strong evidence that two of the hijackers, Satam al Suqami and Abdul Aziz al Omari, when they applied for their visas presented passports that contained fraudulent travel stamps that have been associated with al Qaeda. There is reason to believe that three of the remaining hijackers presented such altered or manipulated passports as well.

- Fifteen of the 19 hijackers were Saudi nationals.

- Two of the Saudi 9/11 hijackers (brothers Waleed and Wail al Shehri) may have obtained their passports legitimately or illegitimately with the help of a family member who worked in the passport office.

- Two of the hijackers were issued visas in Berlin; two were issued visas in the United Arab Emirates. The remaining 15 were issued a total of 18 visas in Saudi Arabia, 14 of which were issued in Jeddah (11 by the same consular officer), and 4 in Riyadh.[204]

- Of the 23 hijacker visa applications, five were destroyed routinely along with other documents before 9/11 and before their significance was known. The visa applications of Nawaf al Hazmi, Khalid al Mihdhar (in 1999), Mohamed Atta, Marwan al Shehhi, and Ziad Jarrah were destroyed.

- All 19 of the still-existing hijacker applications were incomplete in some way, with a data field left blank or not answered fully.

- Twenty-two of the 23 hijacker applications were approved.[205]

- Only two of the hijackers appear to have been interviewed at the visa stage.

- Of the 15 Saudi hijackers, 4 acquired their visas after the creation of the Visa Express Program in June 2001.

- Eight other conspirators in the plot attempted to acquire U.S. visas during the course of the plot; three of them succeeded.

- Of the three who succeeded, one was Khalid Sheikh Mohammed, the mastermind of the 9/11 plot, who obtained a visa in Jeddah, Saudi Arabia, in July 2001 under an alias. The other two who succeeded were Mushabib al Hamlan, who ultimately did not participate, and Mohamed al Kahtani, who was refused entry into the United States.

- Of the five conspirators who failed to obtain visas   Tawfiq bin Attash (Khallad), Ramzi Binalshibh, Saeed al Ghamdi, Zakariya Essabar, and Ali Abdul Aziz Ali none were denied because consular officials believed they were potential terrorists. They were denied visas either because consular officials believed they might be intending immigrants or because they had failed to submit documents supporting their application.

- Of these conspirators who failed to obtain visas, two were Yemeni, one was Moroccan, one was a Pakistani, and one was a Saudi. Their visa applications were denied in Yemen, Saudi Arabia, the United Arab Emirates, and Germany.

- In summary, a total of 27 individuals   hijackers and other conspirators attempted to obtain visas during the course of the 9/11 plot. These individuals submitted a total of 35 applications. Of these, 25 were approved.

---

[1] Hani Hanjour was the first 9/11 hijacker to acquire a U.S. visa and come to the United States. He entered four times before September 11, three times to seek a U.S. education. Immigration records for Hanjour

indicate that he acquired a B-2, or tourist, visa in Saudi Arabia before traveling to the United States in September 1991 and March 1996. Records of Hanjour's earlier visa applications were destroyed at the Jeddah post. DOS memo from Richard Baltimore, Consul General, Jeddah, Saudi Arabia, Nov. 28, 2001, describing a search that recovered "all applications and documents available on file relating to issuance of their [the 9/11 hijackers'] visas," and stating that Hanjour's earliest application was his 1997 visa application. See also Consular Officer No. 5 interview (Mar. 2, 2004), describing how, generally, Jeddah post kept visa applications for two years. Hanjour entered the United States on these visas within a month of acquiring them on October 3, 1991, and Apr. 2, 1996. There is no record as to when Hanjour left the country after his first visit, although he was permitted a six-month stay. INS record, NIIS record of Hanjour, Oct. 3, 1991 and Apr. 2, 1996.

Hanjour's March 1996 tourist visa was issued with a notation on the application stating "prospective student, school not yet selected." INS record, NIIS record of Hanjour, Apr. 2, 1996 with visa issuance date of Mar. 19, 1996. Records indicate that when Hanjour returned on April 2, 1996, he received another six-month length of stay as a tourist. INS record, NIIS record of Hanjour, Apr. 2, 1996 with length of stay until Oct. 1, 1996. On June 7, 1996, Hanjour filed an INS I-539 application to change his immigration status from tourist to academic student to attend the ELS Language Center in Oakland, California. During this time, Hanjour also had contact with the Caldwell Flight Academy in New Jersey and the Sierra Academy in Oakland. Caldwell Flight Academy record of Hanjour, June 6, 2001, and Sierra Academy of Aeronautics record of Hanjour, Sept. 3, 1996. The application was quickly approved 20 days later, on June 27, 1996, and allowed Hanjour to stay in the United States until May 20, 1997. INS record, I-539 Application to Change Nonimmigrant Status of Hanjour, May 24, 1996. Hanjour attended the Sierra Academy from September 3 to September 9, 1996. Well before his length of stay expired, Hanjour departed the United States in November 1996. INS record, NIIS record of Hanjour April 2, 1996 with date of departure of Nov. 26, 1996.

On his November 1997 visa application, Hanjour answered "no" to the question "Have you ever applied for a U.S. visa before, whether immigrant or nonimmigrant?" He also answered "no" to the question "Have you ever been in the U.S.A.?" DOS record, visa application of Hanjour, Nov. 2, 1997. It is difficult to establish the intent behind these false statements. The application does bear a signature that appears identical to the signature on Hanjour's two 2000 visa applications. DOS record, visa applications of Hanjour, Sept. 10 and Sept. 25, 2000. However, the application form also indicated that it was prepared by "Siddiqi/Samara Travel." DOS record, visa application of Hanjour, Nov. 2, 1997. Thus, the false statements may have been made inadvertently by a travel agent who filled out the form on Hanjour's behalf. The consular officer who adjudicated Hanjour's 1997 visa application interviewed him on November 2, 1997. This officer said that they would interview 50–60 percent of the Saudi applicants. DOS Office of Inspector General Memorandum of Conversation (OIG MOC) with Consular Officer No. 5, Feb. 5, 2003. The officer who interviewed him about his application did not recall many details of the interview, but was able to reconstruct some aspects of it from notes on the visa application. DOS OIG MOC with Consular Officer No. 5, Feb. 5, 2003. The officer said he would not have known about Hanjour's prior travel to the United States unless it was reflected in his passport. The officer also said he could not understand why Hanjour would have sought to cover up prior travel to the United States, adding, "It's perplexing that they would hide that because it works in their favor." Consular Officer No. 5 interview (Mar. 2, 2004). He did say, though, that a Saudi who had been to the United States twice before, as Hanjour apparently had been, and who then applied to go to the United States for English studies would have "raise[d] an eyebrow" because a student visa applicant must demonstrate that he or she has made reasonable progress in their studies. Ibid. The officer said underperforming Saudi students were denied visas on some occasions. Ibid. In general, the officer told us, they felt they could make visa adjudications with only the basic biographical information Saudis typically provided. However, the officer made a point of telling us that "it bothered me; it disturbed me" to accept so many incomplete applications from Saudis. When they raised it at post, they were told by the local staff, "Well, we have always done it this way." Ibid. There is no evidence they sought to raise the question with their superiors.

Hanjour traveled to the United States on November 16, 1997 on that visa and was granted a two-year length of stay by an immigration inspector. The visa allowed Hanjour to attend the ELS Language Centers in Florida. But Hanjour instead began flight training at Cockpit Resource Management Airline Training Center in Scottsdale, Arizona. Seven months later, on June 16, 1998, Hanjour filed an I-539, seeking a change of status from academic student (F-1) to M1 vocational student (M-2) to attend the

Cockpit Resource Management from July 30, 1998 to July 29, 1999. Eight months later, the INS asked Hanjour to supply supporting evidence for his request. INS record, I-539 Application to Change Nonimmigrant Status of Hanjour, June 9, 1998, and INS record, I-539 Notice of Action of Hanjour, June 16, 1998. The application was not approved until Jan. 16, 2001, for a retroactive length of stay from July 30, 1998, to July 29, 1999. Having attended the flight school and received a commercial pilot's license from the Federal Aviation Administration (FAA) in April 1999 without ever receiving INS approval to change his status, Hanjour left the country that month. For flight school attendance and FAA approval, see Penttbom Summary, Feb. 29, 2004. INS record, NIIS record of Hanjour, Nov. 16, 1997, with a departure date of April 28, 1999. His I-539 was not approved until January 16, 2001. By that point, Hanjour had already acquired a new academic visa and reentered the United States for his last time. DOS record, Visa Application of Hanjour, Sept. 25, 2000; INS record, NIIS record of Hanjour, Dec. 8, 2000.

[2] INS memo, Ken Elwood, Deputy Executive Associate Commissioner, Office of Field Operations to the field, Nov. 11, 1998.

[3] DOS record, NIV Applicant Detail of Nawaf al Hazmi, Nov. 19, 2001.

[4] FBI record, copy of Nawaf al Hazmi's passport.

[5] DOS record, visa application of Salah Saeed Mohammed Bin Yousaf, April 3, 1999.

[6] Ibid.

[7] Ibid. Yemenis has a 66 percent refusal rate for "B" visas in fiscal year 1999. DOS record, "Visa Issuance and Refusal Data for the Country of Yemen," June 18, 2004.

[8] Khallad claims he applied for a visa before the 1999 application. DOS has searched for this application using his real name and known aliases, but has been unable to locate any records supporting this claim. However, the records could have been destroyed and no electronic record retained.

[9] DOS record, NIV Applicant Detail of Khalid al Mihdhar, Nov. 8, 2001; Copy of Khalid al Mihdhar's passport number B721156..

[10] FBI Penttbom Timeline, Dec. 5, 2003.

[11] A consular officer serving in Jeddah at this time told Commission staff that Saudi citizens were considered security risks by Jeddah consular officers, that they interviewed "the majority" of Saudi males between the ages of 16 and 40, and that they were not shy about turning down Saudi male visa applicants on security grounds—including applicants whom the officers felt had no good reason to be going to the United States. This officer told us he would be "shocked" to learn that they had not interviewed Saudi males like Nawaf al Hazmi and Khalid al Mihdhar, who were between 16 and 40 years of age and traveling alone. However, he did not handle their visa applications. Consular Officer No. 12 interview (Feb. 24, 2004).

[12] DOS OIG MOC with Consular Officer No. 6, Feb. 3, 2003.

[13] Although today consular officers typically take notes electronically while interviewing an applicant—notes made part of the permanent CCD record—that was not the case in April 1999.

[14] INS records, NIIS records of Nawaf al Hazmi and Khalid al Mihdhar, Jan. 15, 2000 and primary inspector interviews for both these entries (May 24, 2004).

[15] CIA cable, "Activities of Bin Ladin Associate Khalid Revealed," Jan. 4, 2000.

[16] DOS record, NIV Applicant Detail of Marwan al Shehhi, Nov. 8, 2001.

[17] DOS OIG MOC with Consular Officer No. 7, Feb. 11, 2003.

[18] Ibid.

[19] Consular Officer No. 10 interview (Mar.1, 2004).

[20] DOS record, NIV Applicant Detail of Nawaf al Hazmi, Nov. 19, 2001, with visa expiration date April 2, 2001.

[21] American Association of Motor Vehicle Administrators (AAMVA) memo, "9/11 hijacker driver license and identification paper trail," May 28, 2004.

[22] DOS record, NIV Applicant Detail of Mohamed Atta, May 17, 2000. The hijackers received visas of different lengths dependent on reciprocal agreements in place between the United States and their countries of origin. A copy of Mohamed Atta's U.S. visa is attached in Appendix A.

[23] Consular Officer No. 9 interview (Feb. 20, 2004).

[24] DOS records, visa applications of Ramzi Binalshibh, May 16, June 5, Sept. 15 and Oct. 25, 2000. A copy of the first page of Binalshibh's first visa application is attached in Appendix A.

[25] DOS record, NIV Applicant Detail of Ziad Jarrah, Nov. 8, 2001. Jarrah's original visa application was destroyed, but an electronic record, including his photograph, remains in the State Department's electronic

records. A partly-burned copy of Jarrah's U.S. visa, recovered from the crash scene of Flight 93, is attached in Appendix A.

[26] DOS OIG MOC with Consular Officer No. 8, Feb. 11, 2003.

[27] INS record, NIIS record of Marwan al Shehhi, May 29, 2000, and Customs record, Customs Secondary Inspection Result of Marwan al Shehhi, May 29, 2000.

[28] INS record, NIIS record of Mohamed Atta, June 3, 2000.

[29] Ramzi Binalshibh's NIV Applicant Detail produced to the Commission by the State Department lists the adjudication dates of his Berlin visas as June 5, June 27, July 18, and Nov. 1, 2000.

[30] That provision of law states: "No visa . . . shall be issued to an alien if (1) it appears to the consular officer, from statements in the application, or in the papers submitted therewith, that such alien is ineligible to receive a visa . . . under section 212, or any other provision of law, (2) the application fails to comply with the provisions of this Act, or the regulations issued thereunder, or (3) the consular officer knows or has reason to believe that such alien is ineligible to receive a visa . . . under section 212, or any other provision of law."

[31] DOS regulations, Authority to Require Documents of Visa Applicants, 22 C.F.R. § 41.105(a)(1): "The consular officer is authorized to require documents considered necessary to establish the alien's eligibility to receive a nonimmigrant visa. All documents and other evidence presented by the alien, including briefs submitted by attorneys or other representatives, shall be considered by the consular officer."

[32] 22 CFR § 41.103(b)(2) (additional information as part of application).

[33] Consular Officer No. 9 interview (Feb. 20, 2004); 22 CFR § 41.121 (Refusal of individual visas) provides, "If the ground(s) of ineligibility may be overcome by the presentation of additional evidence, and the applicant has indicated the intention to submit such evidence, a review of the refusal may be deferred for not more then 120 days."

[34] FBI report, "Summary of Penttbom Investigation," Feb. 29, 2004.

[35] INS record, NIIS record of Ziad Jarrah, June 27, 2000.

[36] FBI report, "Summary of Penttbom Investigation," Feb. 29, 2004.

[37] Huffman Aviation enrollment records of Marwan al Shehhi and Mohamed Atta; DOJ OIG Memorandum of Investigation (MOI), interview of company president, Rudi Dekkers, April 10, 2002. Dekkers also stated that Atta and Shehhi had previously attended Jones Aviation in Sarasota, Florida, but were asked to leave that flight school because of their bad attitudes.

[38] DOJ OIG MOI, interview of Rudi Dekkers, Apr. 10, 2002. FBI report of investigation, interview of Sue Costa,, Sept. 15, 2001.

[39] INS record, I-539 Application to Extend Nonimmigrant Status of Nawaf al Hazmi, July 12, 2000.

[40] According to an official in the State Department's Visa Office within the Bureau of Consular Affairs, State records support a conclusion that Binalshibh's first two visa applications amounted to "one case" that was denied on July 18, 2000 under 214(b). The records themselves also support this conclusion. Copies of Binalshibh's visa application show no writing on his June 15, 2000, application. Rather, notes taken on the May 17, 2000, application described the reasons why both applications then pending were denied, and included the dates of June 5 and July 18—both dates of refusals, according to the State computer system. It appears that Binalshibh's two applications were first denied under 221(g) (on June 5 and June 27) without a face-to-face meeting with a consular officer—a common practice in Berlin during this time period; Binalshibh was denied under 214(b)—the more serious denial—only after a formal interview with a consular officer on July 18, 2000. This surmise is supported by a note on Binalshibh's last application, denied November 1, 2000, on which a consular official wrote "two prior refusals"—i.e., one in Berlin and one in Sanaa, Yemen.

[41] FBI report of investigation, interview of Sue Costa, Sept. 15, 2001.

[42] DOS record, Visa Application of Ahmed al Ghamdi, Sept. 3, 2000.

[43] The consular officer's testimony before Congress reflects his misimpression that Hanjour applied for this visa under the Visa Express program. Testimony of Consular Officer No. 3 before the U.S. House of Representatives, Committee on Government Reform, Aug. 1, 2002, p. 38. This error led the officer to state—incorrectly, we believe—that he had denied Hanjour under section 221(g) in order to call him in for an interview. Ibid, pp. 38–39. "I remember that I had refused him for interview, because he had applied for a tourist visa and he said that his reason for going to the United States was to study," the officer recalled.); Ibid, p. 39 (221(g) denial was "for administrative reasons." It meant "No. Come in. I want to talk to you"). In fact, the date Hanjour applied (as shown on his written application) and the date he was denied (as

shown both on the application and on State's electronic records) are the same: September 10, 2000. A copy of Hanjour's September 10, 2000, visa application is attached in Appendix A.

[44] Ibid.

[45] The student coordinator told the FBI that on "one occasion, Atta was very upset with the date of his visa and wanted it changed." Atta did not tell her what upset him about the date or why he wanted the visa date changed. (We assume this reference is to Atta's length of stay.) FBI report of investigation, interview of Nicole Antini, Sept. 13, 2001.

[46] INS record, I-539 Applications to Change Status for Mohamed Atta, undated; and Marwan al Shehhi, Sept. 15, 2000. A copy of al Shehhi's I-539 is attached in Appendix A.

[47] FBI report of investigation, interview of Ivan Chirivella, Sept. 16, 2001.

[48] On his Oct. 25, 2000, visa application, Binalshibh lists the date of his Sanaa visa application as Aug. 12, 2000. However, the application itself is dated Sept. 15, 2000, and the date stamped on the application for the denial is Sept. 16, 2000.

[49] Ibid.

[50] Ibid.

[51] DOS record, NIV Applicant Detail of Hanjour, Nov. 8, 2001. We were unable to interview the primary inspector who admitted Hanjour on Dec. 8, 2000, to determine how the tourist visa may have been changed upon Hanjour's entry at Cincinnati International to an academic student visa entry.

[52] DOS record, visa application of Hamza al Ghamdi, Oct. 17, 2000.

[53] FBI report, "Summary of Penttbom Investigation," Feb. 24, 2004.

[54] DOS OIG MOC with Consular Officer No. 1, Jan. 22, 2003.

[55] DOS record, visa application of Mohand al Shehri, Oct. 23, 2000. A copy of al Shehri's visa application is attached in Appendix A.

[56] DOS OIG MOC with Consular Officer No. 4, Jan. 24, 2003.

[57] Ibid.

[58] DOS record, visa application of Ahmed al Nami, Oct. 28, 2000.

[59] FBI report, "Summary of Penttbom Investigation," Feb. 24, 2004.

[60] DOS record, visa application of Mushabib al Hamlan, Oct. 28, 2000.

[61] INS record, NIIS record of Ziad Jarrah, Oct. 29, 2000.

[62] FBI report of investigation, interview of Sue Costa, Sept. 15, 2001.

[63] FBI report of investigation, interview of Karen Goduto, Sept. 14, 2001.

[64] DOS record, visa application of Ahmad al Haznawi, Nov. 12, 2000. A copy of Haznawi's application is attached in Appendix A.

[65] FBI report, "Summary of Penttbom Investigations," Feb. 24, 2004.

[66] DOS record, visa application record of Saeed al Ghamdi, Nov. 12, 2000. A copy of al Ghamdi's visa application (in which he spelled his last name "al Gamdi") is attached in Appendix A.

[67] DOS record, visa application record of Majed Moqed, Nov. 20, 2000.

[68] DOS OIG MOC with Consular Officer No. 4, Jan. 24, 2003.

[69] Ibid.

[70] DOS record, visa application record of Satam al Suqami, Nov. 21, 2000.

[71] Although Suqami had false travel stamps in his passport as of 9/11, we do not know if these stamps were placed in his passport before or after submission of his visa application, although the dates on some of the false stamps pre-date the date he applied for his visa.

[72] Testimony of Consular Officer Number No. 2 before the House Committee on Government Reform, Aug. 1, 2002.

[73] Ibid.

[74] Customs record, TECS II Private Aircraft Enforcement System record of Ziad Jarrah, Nov. 25, 2000; and customs inspector of Ziad Jarrah on Nov. 25, 2000 interview (May 18, 2004).

[75] INS record, NIIS record of Hani Hanjour, Dec. 8, 2000. On failure to attend school, see FBI report, "Summary of Penttbom Investigation," Feb. 29, 2004.

[76] DOS record, visa application of Zakariya Essabar, Dec. 12, 2004.

[77] FBI report of investigation, interview of Sue Costa, Sept. 15, 2001. At some point during their schooling, Atta and Shehhi were reportedly offered jobs as co-pilots for a new airline, "Flair" by Huffman's president, Rudi Dekkers. FBI draft report of investigation, interview of Nicole Antini, Sept. 13, 2004.

[78] INS record, NIIS record of Mohamed Atta, June 3, 2000, with length of stay until Dec. 2, 2000, and a departure date of May 18, 2000. For the INS abandonment policy, see INS Memorandum of Tom Cook, Acting Assistant Commissioner for Adjudications addressed to all Service Center Directors, District Directors, and Officers in Charge, June 18, 200. It stated: "Service officers are reminded an alien on whose behalf a change of nonimmigrant status has been filed and who travels outside the United States before the request is adjudicated is considered to have abandoned the request for a change of nonimmigrant status. This has been, and remains, the Service's long-standing policy."

[79] INS record, NIIS record of Ziad Jarrah, Jan. 5, 2001.

[80] Primary immigration inspector of Mohamed Atta on Jan. 10, 2001interview (Mar. 25, 2004); DOJ OIG primary immigration inspector interview, Nov. 27, 2001. INS record, Inspection Results Report record of Mohamed Atta, Jan. 10, 2001.

[81] Primary immigration inspector of Mohamed Atta on Jan. 10, 2001 interview (Mar. 25, 2004). INS record, I-94 arrival record of Mohamed Atta, Jan. 10, 2001.

[82] The "VOID" handwritten over top of this stamp is not the handwriting of the primary inspector, according to him. It is likely the handwriting of the secondary inspector, who told the Commission he could not recognize his own handwriting stating: "I've hurt my writing finger too many times and my handwriting keeps changing; couldn't recognize it."

[83] This policy was in contradiction to the stricter language of the INS Field Guidelines, which had specifically delineated business categories for admission. Continued training as a pilot was not within the language of those guidelines.

[84] Secondary immigration inspector of Mohamed Atta on Jan. 10, 2001interview (Mar. 25, 2004); DOJ OIG interview of secondary immigration inspector of Atta on Jan. 10, 2001, Dec. 20, 2001. We asked these questions because under immigration law, "part-time schooling" is considered incidental to the primary purpose of a visit, and did not require a new student visa or a change of status from tourist to student.

[85] Secondary immigration inspector of Mohamed Atta on Jan. 10, 2001interview (Mar. 25, 2004). For the abandonment policy, see INS Tom Cook policy memo stating that pending benefits applications are considered abandoned if the alien leaves while the application is pending, therefore requiring the applicant to attain a visa abroad for that same benefit prior to re-entry. (There is no reference to this policy in the *INS Field Inspectors'* Manual.) In other words, if Atta wanted to study in the United States and filed an application to that effect but left the country while it was pending, he needed to get a student visa abroad in order to return to the United States. The initial application was considered no longer valid. For other inspectors aware of this policy, see Commission interview of inspector for Atta's deferred inspection on May 2, 2001.

[86] Secondary immigration inspector of Mohamed Atta on Jan. 10, 2001interview (Mar. 25, 2004). DOJ OIG interview of secondary immigration inspector of Atta on Jan. 10, 2001, Mar. 21, 2002.

[87] Secondary immigration inspector of Mohamed Atta on Jan. 10, 2001interview (Mar. 25, 2004). Also see Justice Department Inspector General Report, *The INS Contacts with Two September 11 Terrorists*, (May 20, 2002), p. 56-58.

[88] The eight-month time period is recalled by another inspector who reviewed Atta's I-94 arrival record in May 2001, as this inspector changed Atta's length of stay from eight months back to six months. The electronic admission record also noted an eight month stay. The admission stamp, (although hard to read), bares this secondary inspector's number. It appears that the secondary inspector wrote "VOID" on the primary inspector's one month B1 admission stamp in Atta's passport, and instead admitted Atta as a tourist for eight months, apparently to accommodate Atta's schooling. The same handwriting appears on Atta's I-94 arrival record as well, crossing out the primary inspector's one month stay and replacing it with a sloppy handwritten date which looks to be September 8, 2001, with the same length of stay that listed on the original immigration arrival record.

[89] If an alien files an application for a change of status while they are legally in the United States, they may stay in the country until the application is adjudicated. In addition, Atta could have qualified for a deferred inspection if the inspector was convinced that "the case could possibly be resolved in the alien's favor," see INS Field Inspectors' Manual at 17.1.

[90] Secondary immigration inspector of Mohamed Atta on Jan. 10, 2001interview (Mar. 25, 2004).

[91] Commission work product chart, *September 11 Hijacker border inspection interview results: Red Flags Resulting in Secondary Interviews*, May 20, 2004.

[92] On deferred inspections, see INS Field Inspectors' Manual at 17.1.

[93] INS record, NIIS record of Marwan al Shehhi, Jan. 18, 2001.

[94] Primary immigration inspector of Marwan al Shehhi on Jan. 18, 2001 interview (Mar. 26, 2004).

[95] INS record, INS Inspections Results Report record of Marwan al Shehhi, Jan. 18, 2001. In the interview of Marwan al Shehhi's primary immigration inspector , she said: "I referred him to secondary and he didn't want to leave the booth. 'What is your problem?' I said. He simply said, 'No.' I had to get out of the booth and take him into secondary because I thought he would bolt, and I sat him down. I told someone in secondary to watch him. He made me remember him; if he had been smart he wouldn't have done that," see Primary immigration inspector of Marwan al Shehhi on Jan. 18, 2001 interview (Mar. 26, 2004).

[96] Secondary immigration inspector of Marwan al Shehhi on Jan. 18, 2001 interview (Mar. 22, 2004). For length of time Shehhi spent in secondary, see INS record, INS secondary inspection roster for JFK on January 18, 2001, during the time frame Shehhi was referred to secondary.

[97] Secondary immigration inspector of Marwan al Shehhi on Jan. 18, 2001 interview (Mar. 22, 2004).

[98] Ibid.

[99] Ibid.

[100] Ibid. For baseline time given for business visitors at JFK International Airport (the baseline differed amongst the air ports where the hijackers entered, see Commission work product chart, *September 11 Hijacker border inspection interview results: Primary Inspection Procedures Prior to September 11*, May 20, 2004). Also see Commission interviews of three JFK inspectors who had contact with the 9/11 hijackers (March 22, March 25 and May 24, 2004).

[101] INS record, NIIS record of Ziad Jarrah, Jan. 5, 2001 with a departure date of Jan. 26, 2001.

[102] INS record, NIIS record of Ziad Jarrah, Feb. 25, 2001. For baseline time given for business visitors at air ports of entry, see Commission work product chart, *September 11 Hijacker border inspection interview results: Primary Inspection Procedures Prior to September 11*, May 20, 2004.

[103] INS record, NIIS record of Ziad Jarrah, Feb. 25, 2001 with a departure date of March 30, 2001.

[104] AAMVA memo, "9/11 hijacker driver license and identification paper trail," May 28, 2004.

[105] INS record, NIIS record of Ziad Jarrah, April 13, 2001 with a length of stay until July 30, 2001.

[106] On Ahmed al Nami's passports, see DOS record, NIV Applicant Detail for Ahmed al Nami (Nov. 8, 2001).

[107] DOS record, DOS visa application of Ahmed al Nami, April 23, 2001. A copy of al Nami's application is attached in Appendix A.

[108] INS records, I-94 Arrival Records for Waleed al Shehri and Satam al Suqami, Apr. 23, 2001.

[109] The passport was recovered by NYPD Detective Yuk H. Chin from a male passerby in a business suit, about 30 years old. The passerby left before being identified, while debris was falling from WTC 2. The tower collapsed shortly thereafter. The detective then gave the passport to the FBI on 9/11. See FBI report, interview of Detective Chin, Sept. 12, 2001.

[110] Analytic reference report, Apr. 1, 2003. In addition, the Forensic Document Analysis of Satam al Suqami's passport indicates that on page 8, "An Arabic stamp impression located near the top of page 8 has been partially covered with correction fluid," see INS letter from John Ross, INS Supervisory Forensic Document Examiner, to Lorie Gottesman, FBI Document Examiner, Nov. 2, 2001.

[111] Primary immigration inspector of Satam al Suqami interview (Apr. 23, 2001).

[112] INS records, I-94 Arrival Records for Majed Moqed and Ahmed al Ghamdi, May 2, 2001 and Customs record, Customs Declaration for Majed Moqed, May 2, 2001. On the requirement to fill out electronic reports on amounts declared over $10,000, see Rick Colon interview, June 14, 2004.

[113] INS record, NIIS record of Marwan al Shehhi, May 2, 2001 with a length of stay until Nov. 2, 2001.

[114] In regard to the identification of Atta's companions, the inspector identified two of three. She said all three had olive skin tone and dark features. She told the Commission she would never forget Atta, whom she told a colleague was "an ugly man, he looked like a bulldog." The companion who first spoke to the inspector, she recalled "was a great looking kid," which she also mentioned to a colleague. When the FBI's Most Wanted photo of Adnan G. El Shukrijumah appeared on the inspectors' bulletin board after September 11, and after the FBI interviewed her, the inspector says she told her supervisor at the port that she was "75 percent sure" that she could identify the man who was with Atta as Shukrijumah. In checking Shukrijumah's immigration status, she learned that he was a legal resident and had worked in south Florida. Information about the September 11 plot has not to date associated Shukrijumah with the plot. However, Shukrijumah is considered a well-connected al Qaeda operative, otherwise known as "Jafar the Pilot" and he is still wanted by the FBI. Shukrijumah's father is a well known imam in South Florida,

having testified on behalf of Sheik Rahman during his trial for the conspiracy to destroy New York landmarks in June 1993. The inspector cannot recall what the third companion looked like, and did not recognize any of the photos of other hijackers shown to her. The Commission, however, believes that Jarrah may have been one of Atta's companions. He was the only hijacker who matched the facts as told by the inspector, that Atta's "friend" had come back in January and received a six month stay. It is also known that Jarrah was with Atta later that day, driving north to get a Florida driver's license. See immigration inspector of Mohamed Atta on May 2 interview (Mar. 25, 2004).

[115] See immigration inspector of Mohamed Atta on May 2 interview (Mar. 25, 2004).

[116] Ibid.

[117] Ibid.

[118] Ibid.; a copy of Atta's May 2, 2001, INS record (I-94) is attached in Appendix A.

[119] AAMVA memo, "9/11 hijacker driver license and identification paper trail," May 28, 2004. A copy of Atta's Florida Driver License is attached in Appendix A.

[120] Ibid.

[121] Ibid.

[122] Intelligence report, interrogation of detainee, Apr. 2, 2004.

[123] For departure date of May 16, 2001, INS record, Immigrant Admission Information of Satam al Suqami, Sept. 14, 2001and INS record, NIIS record of Waleed al Shehri, Apr. 23, 2001 with a departure date of May 16, 2001. There was a mistake on Shehri's port of departure on this record, however, stating that he left from Fall River, Massachusetts, as opposed to Fort Lauderdale. An FBI phone interview indicates that an immigration inspector in Freeport, Bahamas checked the local immigration records and noted that the two arrived together on Gulfstream Continental flight 9273 at 8:20 am. FBI report of investigation, interview of Freeport, Bahamas immigration inspector, Sept. 18, 2001.

[124] Interrogation of Ramzi Binalshibh, Apr. 7, 2004.

[125] FBI report of investigation, interview of Freeport, Bahamas immigration inspector, Sept. 18, 2001.

[126] Preclearance stations existed prior to September 11 in Canada, Ireland, the Bahamas and the Caribbean.

[127] Customs record, Secondary Inspection record of Waleed al Shehri, May 16, 2001. The attempted three-day jaunt by Shehri and Suqami to the Bahamas would cause difficulty for the INS in assisting the FBI's investigation into 9/11 since the INS records indicated the two had left the United States and not returned. This is because when the two left Miami for the Bahamas, they handed in their I-94 departure records as required. When they were turned around in the Bahamas for a lack of visas, under U.S. immigration law they never left the United States. However, they were not given new arrival records when they physically returned to the United States. Therefore, when the attacks occurred, investigators thought that Suqmai and Shehri had departed the U.S., which is what the INS records indicated.

[128] DOJ record, "Hijacker Identity Documents: Passports, Visas, Licenses/Identification Cards."

[129] Nami obtained a Florida driver's license, but we do not know when. AAMVA memo, "9/11 hijacker driver license and identification paper trail," May 28, 2004.

[130] INS records, I-94 Arrival Records of Hamza al Ghamdi, Mohand al Shehri, and Ahmed al Nami, May 28, 2001.

[131] DOS record, DOS cable from the Embassy Riyadh to Secretary of State, Aug. 19, 2001.

[132] INS records, NIIS records for Ahmad al Haznawi and Wail al Shehri, June 8, 2001.

[133] DOS record, NIV Applicant Detail of Saeed al Ghamdi, Aug. 12, 2002.

[134] DOS record, Visa Application of Saeed al Ghamdi, Nov. 19, 2001.

[135] Ibid.

[136] DOS record, visa application of Khalid al Mihdhar, June 13, 2001, and a digital image of Khalid al Mihdhar's C551754 passport.

[137] DOS record, visa application of Abdul Aziz al Omari, June 18, 2001.

[138] DOS record, DOS visa application of Fayez Banihammad, June 18, 2001.

[139] Consular Officer No. 10 interview (Mar.1, 2004).

[140] FBI memo from Legat Riyadh, "Penttbom case," Oct. 25, 2001.

[141] DOJ, "Hijacker Identity Documents: Passports, Visas, Licenses/Identification Cards."

[142] See CIA analytic reference report, "A Reference Guide for Terrorist Passports," Feb. 14, 2003.

[143] Testimony of Consular Officer Number No. 2 before the House Committee on Government Reform, Aug. 1, 2002.

[144] Ibid.

[145] AAMVA memo, "9/11 hijacker driver license and identification paper trail," May 28, 2004.

[146] Ibid.

[147] INS records, NIIS records of Fayez Banihammad and Saeed al Ghamdi, June 27, 2001.

[148] INS record, I-94 Arrival Record and Customs record, Customs Declaration of Fayez Banihammad, June 27, 2001. For admission of Banihammad, see primary immigration inspector for Fayez Banihammad interview (May 19, 2004).

[149] Primary immigration inspector of Saeed al Ghamdi interview (Mar. 17, 2004). This inspector did not know that a September 11 hijacker came through his line until a colleague had told him a few months prior to the Commission's interview request. Most of the inspectors we interviewed were not aware they had adjudicated the entrance of a 9/11 hijacker.

[150] INS record, INS Inspection Results record of Saeed al Ghamdi, June 27, 2001.

[151] Customs record, Customs Declaration record of Saeed al Ghamdi, June 27, 2001 and primary immigration inspector of Saeed al Ghamdi interview (Mar. 17, 2004). Copies of Ghamdi's Customs Declaration and I-94 are attached in Appendix A.

[152] INS record, INS Inspection Results record of Saeed al Ghamdi, June 27, 2001and primary immigration inspector of Saeed al Ghamdi interview (Mar. 17, 2004). The Commission cannot verify whether Ghamdi's travel documents were clean since no copies survived the attacks or were recovered elsewhere.

[153] INS records, I-94 Arrival Records of Abdul Aziz al Omari and Salem al Hazmi, June 29, 2001.

[154] CIA analytic reference report, Apr.1, 2003.

[155] FBI record, Penttbom Major Case # 182, DOCEX document, undated.

[156] DOJ document, "Hijacker Identity Documents: Passports, Visas, Licenses/Identification Cards," undated.

[157] AAMVA memo, "9/11 hijacker driver license and identification paper trail," May 28, 2004. A copy of Salem al Hazmi's USA ID document is attached in Appendix A.

[158] USSS report, "Physical examination of identifications of 'Salem Alhazmi' and 'Alhazmi' found at the Pentagon, Sept. 25 and 27, 2001.

[159] AAMVA memo, "9/11 hijacker driver license and identification paper trail," May 28, 2004.

[160] INS record, I-94 Arrival Record of Khalid al Mihdhar, July 4, 2001.

[161] Commission work product chart, *September 11 Hijacker border inspection interview results: Primary Inspection Procedures Prior to September 11*, May 20, 2004.

[162] A digital copy of Mihdhar's passport was recovered during a search of an al Qaeda safehouse.

[163] Primary immigration inspector for Khalid al Mihdhar interview (May 24, 2001).

[164] DOS record, visa application record of Mohammad al Kahtani, July 4, 2001 and DOS record, NIV Applicant Detail for Mohammad al Kahtani, Jan. 16, 2004.

[165] Veronica Cates interview (May 25, 2004); Rocky Concepcion interview (June 15, 2004); Rick Colon interview (June 14, 2004); Dan Cadman interview (June 14, 2004); and Kevin Rooney interview (Jan. 8, 2004).

[166] Veronica Cates interview (May 25, 2004); Rocky Concepcion interview (June 15, 2004); Rick Colon interview (June 14, 2004); Dan Cadman interview (June 14, 2004); Kevin Rooney interview (Jan. 8, 2004).

[167] Customs record, TECS II-Administrative Message record, July 6, 2001; and Rick Colon interview (June 14, 2004).

[168] INS record, NIIS record of Mohamed Atta, Jan. 10, 2001, with departure date of July 7, 2001 and length of stay until July 9, 2001.

[169] DOJ dcument, "Hijacker Identity Documents: Passports, Visas, Licenses/Identification Cards," undated.

[170] AAMVA memo, "9/11 hijacker driver license and identification paper trail," May 28, 2004. A copy of Mihdhar's USA ID is attached in Appendix A.

[171] INS record, INS I-539 Application to Change Status of Mohamed Atta, undated.

[172] INS record, I-94 Arrival Record of Mohamed Atta, July 19, 2001.

[173] Primary immigration inspector of Mohamed Atta on July 19, 2001 interview (May 17, 2004).

[174] DOS record, NIV Applicant Detail record of Khalid Sheikh Mohammad under alias of Abdulrahman AA Al Ghamdi, Jan. 13, 2004. A copy of KSM's U.S. visa application is attached as Appendix A.

[175] DOS record, visa application of Khalid Sheikh Mohammad under alias of Abdulrahman AA Al Ghamdi, July 23, 2001.

[176] DOS record, NIV Applicant Detail of Saeed al Ghamdi, Nov. 19, 2001.

[177] United States v. Kenys A. Galicia, U.S.D.C.E.D. Va., Oct. 2001 term, Indictment, Paragraphs 7, 8, Oct. 25, 2001.

[178] United States v. Luis A. Martinez-Flores, Affidavit in Support of a Criminal Complaint and an Arrest Warrant, E.D.Va, Sept. 28, 2001.

[179] See Martinez-Flores and Galicia cases.

[180] For Moqed's use of the same address, see Virginia Department of Motor Vehicles Residency Form DL51 for Majed Moqed, Aug. 2, 2001.

[181] Virginia Department of Motor Vehicles Residency Form DL51 for Ziad Jarrah, with residency certified by Hani Hanjour, Aug. 29, 2001. Hanjour used as his address the same address he had fraudulently obtained on Aug. 1, 2001. Jarrah's listed address is fictitious.

[182] United States v. Herbert Villalobos, Affidavit in Support of a Criminal Complaint and an Arrest Warrant, E.D.Va.

[183] AAMVA memo, "9/11 hijacker driver license and identification paper trail," May 28, 2004. In addition, Hanjour had also acquired Arizona and Florida driver's licenses in 1991 and 1996, respectively. A copy of Ahmed al Ghamdi's Virginia identification document is attached in Appendix A.

[184] INS record, I-94 Arrival Record of Mohammad al Kahtani, Aug. 4, 2001, with "Application Withdrawn to Depart Foreign Under Safeguard" stamped on the record. Also see INS record, Withdrawal of Application for Admission/Consular Notification of Mohammad al Kahtani, Aug. 4, 2001.

[185] A combination of evidence gathered by the FBI supports this conclusion: vehicle rental records for Atta during this time period; parking records for this vehicle at Orlando International Airport during the time frame in which Kahtani was attempting entry; and phone records from a public phone to a phone number associated with both Atta and Kahtani. FBI record, Documentation Sufficient to show Mohamed Atta's Presence at the Orlando International Airport on August 4, 2001, including rental vehicle, parking and calling card records, Aug. 11, 2003.

[186] Primary immigration inspector of Mohammed Kahtani interview, April 18, 2004.

[187] Jose Melendez-Perez testimony, Jan. 26, 2004. INS headquarters had previously interviewed the secondary inspector on a couple of occasions. However, no one from the FBI or intelligence community spoke to this inspector or to the primary inspector prior to Commission interviews.

[188] Ibid.

[189] Ibid.

[190] We compared the copy of Kahtani's passport with the U.S. Government publication Counterfeit Travel Stamp Directory (Dec. 2003).

[191] CIA cable to DOS, INS, FBI, and Customs, Aug. 23, 2001.

[192] Customs records, TECS II records of Nawaf al Hazmi and Khalid al Mihdhar, Aug. 24, 2001.

[193] DOS record, visa application of Ali Abdul Aziz Ali, Aug. 27, 2004 and DOS record, NIV Applicant Detail of Ali Abdul Aziz Ali, Jan. 13, 2004.

[194] AAMVA memo, "9/11 hijacker driver license and identification paper trail," May 28, 2004.

[195] Ibid.

[196] FBI record, Customs Service information on TECS II database review of Khalid al Mihdhar, Sept. 12, 2001.

[198] INS record, Lookout Inquiry record for Khalid al Mihdhar, Sept. 4, 2001.

[199] AAMVA memo, "9/11 hijacker driver license and identification paper trail," May 28, 2004.

[200] FBI Report of investigation, Customs Service information on Khalid al Mihdhar, Sept. 12, 2001. The Commission was unable to locate the text of the lookout explaining what action the inspector should have taken.

[201] AAMVA memo, "9/11 hijacker driver license and identification paper trail," May 28, 2004.

[202] FBI records of airline personnel indicate that some recall specific hijackers presenting U.S. identification documents with their airline tickets. The American Airlines ticket agent at Logan Airport recalls the al Shehri brothers presenting drivers' licenses at check-in. FBI report of investigation, Elvia C., Sept. 13, 2001. When Hamza al Ghamdi and Ahmed al Ghamdi checked in at Logan Airport in Boston, Hamza al Ghamdi used his Florida driver's license and Ahmed al Ghamdi used his fraudulently obtained Virginia identification card. FBI report of investigation, interview of Gail J., Sept. 21, 2001. At Dulles, Khalid al Mihdhar and Majed Moqed provided their fraudulently obtained Virginia identification cards at the ticket counter. FBI report of investigation, interview of Susan S., American Airline ticketing agent,

Sept. 13, 2001. A "Kingdom of Saudi Arabia Student Identity Card" was found in the rubble at the Pentagon with Moqed's name on it. Forensic examination indicated that it may have been fraudulent. United States Secret Service Forensic Services report for the FBI PENTTBOM investigation regarding the physical examination of forensic science research request, Oct. 10, 2001. Hijackers Omari, Wail al Shehri and Hanjour also had international driver licenses and Jarrah had an international student identification card.

[203] FBI report of investigation, interview of Caprice C., Sept. 13, 2001. She was employed as a ticket agent by American Airlines at Logan Airport on September 11, 2001.

[204] This sum does not include Hanjour's 1997 visa application in Jeddah because this pre-dates the plot.

[205] Hanjour's second application in September 2000 was approved after he supplied additional paperwork.

www.ingramcontent.com/pod-product-compliance
Lightning Source LLC
Chambersburg PA
CBHW081801280526

45789CB00008B/2945